A Gardener Weeds God's Creation

- a 30 day devotional -

by
Reverend George Kaufinger

FOUR-G Publishers, Inc.
1996

Copyright © 1996
by George Kaufinger

All rights reserved. No part of this volume may be reproduced in any form or by any means without the written permission, in advance, of the author.

FOUR-G Publishers Cataloging-in-Publication

Kaufinger, George.
 A gardener weeds God's creation : a 30-day devotional /
by George Kaufinger. -- Winter Park, FL : FOUR-G Pubs, 1996.
 160 pages ; 23 cm.

 1. Devotional calendars. 2. Devotional exercises.
 I. Title.

   BV4811.K39 1996
   ISBN: 1885066-20-1

Copies of this book are available from:

Reverend George Kaufinger
1623 Yeoman's Path
Lakeland, Florida 33809
TEL: (941) 853-3545

FOUR-G Publishers, Inc.
P. O. Box 2249,
Winter Park, FL 32790
(407) 679-9331

Printed in the UNITED STATES OF AMERICA

TABLE OF CONTENTS
WITH
THOUGHTS FOR THE DAY

DAY   **SUBJECT**

1   **The Importance Of A Garden** 1
God is a gardener. Utilizing gardens, He has revealed His great love for us.

2   **Rebellion Brings Difficulties** 6
Rebellion against God brings difficulties into one's life, as evidenced by the difficulties experienced in raising a productive, eye-pleasing garden.

3   **Nothing Is Useless** 11
Useless things may give us the most profound lesson. Let us listen carefully before we ignore them.

4   **A Question Of Morality** 16
When the chips are down, where do we look for answers regarding moral decisions? Do we accept God's Word or do we react according to our human nature?

5   **Keeping The Garden** 20
Destruction comes from unsuspected directions. We need to be always on the alert in keeping our garden against attack.

6   **Broken Fences Need Replacing** 25
Fences grow old and need to be kept in repair. Failure to replace established fences can ruin any garden.

7   Learn From The Weeds **30**
Weeds are the most important plants in the garden. They teach necessary and vital lessons about eternal truths.

8   God Saw It All **35**
God planned His creation and foresaw all the problems man would create for Him. He still proceeded, knowing He could overcome all the problems.

9   Humans Are Four Dimensional **40**
Humans have four basic needs. When we see and feed only three, we wander off the path God has designed and destruction is around the corner.

10   Weak Roots Are Hard To Destroy **45**
Some sins appear to be easy to destroy. Yet, their roots may continue to linger, and begin to grow when we least expect them.

11   Pockets Of Sin Require Tough Medicine **50**
Little pockets of sin provide the breeding grounds for a whole mess of trouble. Left untouched, they will soon start to dominate our lives.

12   Weeding Should Be Contagious **55**
The example we set may not be readily apparent. Nevertheless, over time it will take effect, and the gardens of sin in the lives of others will be weeded.

13   Good Plants Need Pruning **60**
Plants that produce abundantly can be made to increase their yield through pruning. God, likewise, increases the fruitfulness of our lives by carefully pruning away those branches which hinder the growth of more fruit.

14 **Radical Treatment Brings Hope** 65
Valuable bushes may need to be cut down when disease hits. However, they have a will to live and will spring forth in new growth. All is not lost. Hope is eternal.

15 **Legal But Not Profitable** 70
Our Christian growth is measured by how well we fulfill our responsibilities to our brothers and sisters in Christ, not by the legality of our action.

16 **Weed Seeds Don't Mix Well** 75
Good mulch requires a distinction to be made about the material going into it. Individuals and the church need to separate from the bad in order to ensure adequate growth and preservation of the truth of the Gospel.

17 **Dead Plants Bring Forth Abundantly** 80
Plants, allowed to decay and become mulch, provide the food for new growth. The new creature in Christ must be fed properly. The best food is the decayed, old nature.

18 **Gardens Reveal The Existence Of God** 85
God has expressed Himself in all of creation. Observing the garden, we understand a little of what God is like. It humbles us to know He included us in His plan.

19 **Some Plants Fail To Produce** 90
We plant fruit trees expecting to reap a harvest. The Lord plants souls hoping to reap a similar harvest. Only His patience keeps Him from hewing down unfruitful trees.

20 **Neglect Just Happens** 95
Plants die as a result of neglect. Christian growth dies in the same manner. In the end, our garden and God's garden loses some of its beauty.

21 **God's Gift To Plants** 100
Through the diversity of plant reproduction we have further evidence of creation. It is another way God has attempted to reveal Himself to mankind.

22 **Straight Lines Are Much Nicer** 105
To make straight lines, we have to use some type of guideline. In our spiritual life, the guideline is the Lord Jesus. We make our paths according to His life.

23 **Field Corn Isn't Sweet Corn** 110
We can package a product attractively, but the product may be lacking in quality. Christ is concerned about how we package His gospel. He wants sweetness on the inside, not high-tech designed packages.

24 **Eggplants Need Warm Feet** 115
Eggplants have to have warm feet in order to grow. Christians require the same condition. Proper warming will result in a bumper crop.

25 **Weeds Can Be Very Sneaky** 120
Weeds are tricky. They have cleverly devised ways of ensuring their existence and destructive abilities. False prophets are equally as clever.

26 **Garnering Sheaves Is Hard Work** 125
Hard work often goes unnoticed by our fellow man. Nevertheless, the Ruler of the Universe has seen and our reward will be in proportion to our faithfulness.

27 **Blackberry Thorns Hurt** 130
Blackberry thorns have to be endured, if we are to pick this delectable fruit. The fruits of a deep faith in Christ, are likewise obtained, as we bear the thorns of life.

28   Try And Get The Last Weed 135
We can weed until our hearts are content, and the next day we'll find another weed. Growing in righteousness is very similar: there is always one more weed sin to pull. Lessons learned in childhood will help us in pulling those weeds.

29   Weeding Is Lonely Work 140
People never volunteer to help a gardener weed. Yet, they appreciate the beauty of the garden. Weeding sin from our lives can be lonely work, however, the Trinity will appreciate the beauty and reward us accordingly.

30   Autumn Is A Matter Of Perspective 145
How we view the end of the growing season depends on the perspective we have regarding its meaning. Our spiritual life is also affected by perspective. Where our eyes are focused determines our every action.

BIBLE VERSES BY THE DAY 150

BIBLE VERSES BY THE BOOK 152

DEDICATION

I dedicate this book to my parents, who at an early age instilled in me a love for gardening. From the time I was able to pick up stones, my parents had me in the garden with them. I may not always have been an agreeable participant, but over time I came to appreciate the joy of growing one's vegetables, and the beauty a flower bed can provide. From them, I learned the necessity for hard work and a desire to provide for one's family. Over the years, these qualities have stood me in good stead.

God knew what He was doing when he created the Garden of Eden. He instilled into man from the start of creation an appreciation for growing plants. The first task given to Adam and Eve was to tend the Garden. God knew it would be a satisfying experience. Later, when he had to curse the earth, He still required man to be a gardener in order to provide sustenance.

Every house Loretta and I have owned has provided me the opportunity to participate in the enjoyment, relaxation, and thrill of seeing plants come to fruition. Even vacations have found us touring gardens. They have always provided peace and relaxation.

Had I not been blessed with parents who loved gardening, I may never have come to appreciate the fullness of God's blessings and lessons as found in plants. Mom and Dad, I thank you.

Day 1
THE IMPORTANCE OF A GARDEN

And the Lord God formed man of the dust of the ground, and breathed into his nostrils the breath of life; and man became a living soul. And the Lord God planted a garden eastward in Eden; and there he put the man whom he had formed. And out of the ground made the Lord God to grow every tree that is pleasant to the sight and good for food... (Genesis 2:7-9a)

Thought for the day:
God is a gardener. Utilizing gardens, He has revealed His great love for us.

Gardens play an extremely important part in God's program, for God has chosen the garden as one of the primary ways to manifest His grand design. Lessons contained in the garden cover the whole scheme of God's plan for man, including his redemption. We gardeners are extremely honored by being allowed to experience God's plans in such a wonderful way.

Isn't it interesting how God proceeded in Creation? After He had created all plant and animal life, the final creative act was the creation of man. While the Bible tells us He created man on the sixth day and rested on the seventh, there was one other activity sandwiched between those events. God planted a garden!

Man the supreme creative act was not left to gather his food by foraging the wilderness. God planted a perfect, beautiful, and productive garden. As noted in the above passage, it was in the east part of Eden.

Most of us tend to think of Eden as being the dwelling place of Adam and Eve. However, the garden they dwelt in was only a portion of Eden. Eden covered a large amount of territory according to the Biblical description. Eden wasn't good enough for man so God planted a garden and put man in it. He wanted to give Man a very special dwelling place. God must have taken great pride in this creation He had made. Everything God made was good, but Man needed a special garden planted by God for his existence.

Being a gardener, I find it very heart-warming to reminisce about God planting a garden just for Adam and Eve. It demonstrated the personal love He had for the individuals He had created. I'm sure the garden east of Eden was not a plot forty feet square. It contained all kinds of trees and plants for food and for beauty. It even had special trees called the tree of life, and the tree of knowledge of good and evil. It would have been the most beautiful, bountiful garden ever known. He poured out His love in a most precious way. Father went to a great length to demonstrate His love.

There was another garden at another time where God demonstrated His love. It was on a hill called Golgotha. Part of the hill was used for execution by crucifixion. It was located where the populace could see the executions and be forewarned. However, there was another part of the hill where a garden existed. This garden was used for burying the dead. One day it received a very special body — the body of Jesus, the Son of God. It was another example of the extremes God will execute in order to express His love. What a great love He exemplified by His willingness to sacrifice His own Son for His fallen creatures.

In this demonstration of love, I think there is a second close relationship between the Garden of Eden and the Garden on Golgotha. It concerns God's willingness to use circumstances at both ends of life's spectrum to demonstrate His love. In Eden, He used all the trees good for life and beauty. In Golgotha, He used a place called "Skull" and a garden for the dead. If God can't attract us by providing food and beauty, He will try cruelty and death. God must express His love.

There was even a third garden God utilized in expressing His love. It was called the Garden of Gethsemane. In the Garden, Jesus prayed fervently for the Father to allow the cup of suffering to pass from Him. Three times the Father refused to grant the request of His most Beloved Son. God's love was so great for His fallen creation, He deliberately ignored the pleas of His Son in order to send Him to the cross for the rebellious ones. What a tremendous love God has for His creation, even when they are far removed from His grand design for them.

A second incident occurred in Gethsemane which demonstrated God's love. This was poured out toward His Son. While Jesus was praying in great distress, sweating great drops of blood, God allowed an angel to come and minister to His Son. He understood the agony behind Jesus' appeal. Even though He had to refuse His request, He wanted His Son to know He cared and understood. He would be with Him and see Him through the ordeal.

Often times when personal struggles seem more than I can bear, I go work in my garden. While there, I think about the Garden of Gethsemane and the angel ministering to Christ. Just as the angel came to Christ in Gethsemane, Father comes to me in my garden of trials. The burdens become more bearable. The dark tunnel brightens. God understands my pain and suffering. He cares about my struggles. He will be with me and see me through the ordeal.

We are also called to the Garden of Golgotha. It is no easier to approach than it was for Jesus. It calls for us to crucify self. Pride, lust, bitterness, desires, faithlessness, rebellion, independence do not die easily. Our emotions, will, and mental training are all God given, yet continually want to go in a different direction from their God intended purpose. In each of us there are the attitudes of an Adam, a Cain, a Balaam, a Saul. These attitudes must be crucified.

Christ was crucified once. We must die daily. Each morning on rising, all of the old man tries to resurrect itself and take charge. The most dangerous of attitudes are only a split second away from rising up and taking charge of our lives. A moment of weakness, Satanic enticement, or laxity in watching over our attitudes will quickly result in sin. It was very easy for both Eve and Adam to sin. They slipped into it so easily I am sure they didn't even realize the consequences they were about to incur. The same is true of us. Constantly, Jesus calls us to take up our cross daily and follow him to the garden on Golgotha. There we are to crucify ourselves.

I am so glad, God has given me the privilege of being a gardener. I am more thankful for the gardens He utilized in the Bible to demonstrate His love. They reach down inside and touch my soul and spirit.

Working in my garden I can see the Garden of Eden and its blessings. It reminds me God wants to bless and provide for me. Next, I can see Garden of Gethsemane and I know God cares about my struggles. He is ever ready to minister to me, even though it is His will for me to go through the trial. Finally, I can look into the Garden of Golgotha and know He sacrificed His Son for me because He loved me. I am renewed in spirit and strengthened to go to the cross and crucify a little more of self.

Three beautiful gardens. Three great demonstrations of God's love. Three ways God is using to reach into my life and call me to draw closer to Him. What a great wisdom God possesses. He is due my all.

Father, I thank you for the three gardens you utilized to demonstrate your great love. May they always come to mind as I toil in my garden. I am so appreciative of the teaching you provide in my garden. It means so much to have a place where your great lessons can be made vividly real. I appreciate you so very much. Your love and wisdom are beyond comprehension. Thank you Father. I praise you in Jesus' name. Amen.

DAY 2
REBELLION BRINGS DIFFICULTIES

> *Cursed is the ground for thy sake; in sorrow shalt thou eat of it all the days of thy life; ...and thou shalt eat the herb of the field; ...In the sweat of thy face shalt thou eat bread, till thou return unto the ground;*
> (Genesis 3:17b, 18b, 19a)

Thought for the day:
Rebellion against God brings difficulties into one's life, as evidenced by the difficulties experienced in raising a productive, eye-pleasing garden.

The first two humans on the face of the earth had disobeyed one simple command. It was the only "don't" given them in the Garden of Eden. They were forbidden to eat the fruit of the tree of good and evil. In Adam and Eve, as in all mankind, there was an independent streak saying, "I'll do whatever I please. No one is going to tell me what to do!" It has ever been, and as long as man remains in an unredeemed state, it will be the same in the future. Our hearts are rebellious and independent. They will not willingly surrender to another.

God, in His infinite wisdom, had made man with an independent trait. Throughout the creation account, as God completed each individual act of Creation, He pronounced it good. At the end of the sixth day, God beheld His total creation and pronounced it very good. Man's independence was a characteristic He wanted man to possess. It was part of His crowning achievement in bringing all things into being.

The Creator could have made man like the beasts of the field. They live a programmed life of existence. For each given specie, their lives are a monotonous routine. They always eat the same food, reside in the same environment, follow the same seasonal patterns their genre has always followed. They have a very limited ability to think. They cannot create anything new. Conversation is limited to simple life sustaining sounds for finding food and preservation of the species. God created hundreds of different kinds of pre-programmed non-plant life. To create one more shaped like man would not have been impossible to Him. However, He wanted man to be different. Man was not going to follow a robot life style. Man was going to be given a freedom the other creatures did not possess.

God, the Master Creator, decided man would possess the greatest of all characteristics -- the ability to exercise a will free of any set pattern of action. Creatures made in the image of God had to possess a rational mind. They had to think, weigh options, choose patterns of action, execute those options. Anything less would only cause man to be a robot. He would not have been the supreme end of God's creative acts.

A creature with a free will would be a difficult creature to interface with. There would always be the possibility He would not want to have fellowship with His Creator, be obedient to His laws, or communicate with Him in any way. Nevertheless, it could become the crowning achievement of an intelligent God. If a rational individual could be brought into being, and if that being would willingly surrender himself to his Creator, the wisdom of God would be manifested and honored by His total creation.

Very quickly, man demonstrated to God his perverseness. Not just one, but both humans rebelled against God.

One chose to follow Satan, the other to follow his mate. In the fall, we have manifested the primary ways man will choose. He will listen to Satan and satisfy his own desires, or he will follow some individual, rather than be obedient to his Creator. It is a sad commentary on the capability of man to exercise his free will in a responsible manner.

An omniscient God decided He would demonstrate to man what rebellion brings into life. Man, no longer would be able to enjoy a life of ease. Instead, it would be through difficulty he would obtain the necessary provisions for life. He would struggle with raising productive crops. There would be droughts, famine, sweat, and toil. A life of Edenic bliss was exchanged for a life of toil. Surely intelligent man would understand this object lesson.

Reflection reveals how little man understands this primary, and greatest of all object lessons. His rebellion has been on display for several millenniums. It is still on display today. Man continues to rebel. He continues to struggle to provide for his basic necessities. Walk the streets of our cities and see the homeless. Turn on the television set and see the starving masses in Africa and Russia. Pick up a business publication and read the troubles being encountered by the large multi-national corporations. Read the daily paper and comprehend how we are destroying our environment. Man's rebellion continues to bring massive problems.

Those of us who are fortunate to be gardeners experience God's object lesson in the same way the first humans experienced it. We must spend hours in work to produce a crop of good vegetables or a flower garden of real beauty. There is planting, weeding, hoeing, feeding, insects, blight, foraging animals, transplanting, watering, and frost to be coped with on almost a daily basis. Just as a particular plant is coming into fruition, it may suddenly die. Other times, healthy appearing plants fail to produce the abundance one would expect. It is by the sweat of our face, we experience the consequences of rebellion.

I often think of Adam and Eve when I'm in my garden. I very quickly blame them for all the work I'm experiencing. Then, I stop and realize it wasn't only their rebellion which caused the problem. I have the same attitude active in my life. My free will allows me to easily follow the dictates of my desires, or the trends of my fellow man. Rather than seeking God's will, I can easily push Him into the background. Courses of action are taken which only bring adverse consequences into my life.

With all of the teachings of the Bible, the evidence of the world's struggle in our daily news media, and the struggles I face in my garden, one would think I would have learned a lesson by now. Yet, I know the perverseness of my heart. I am just as incapable of putting God first in my life as were Adam and Eve and the tens of thousands since time began. I may be a Christian, but at heart I am still a rebel.

Pride often says, "George you would never have done what Adam and Eve did." It is at those times, I think of my garden and the struggles I face with it. Quickly, I am humbled. The garden is there as a constant reminder of my rebelliousness. God, in His infinite wisdom, provided a beautiful way of manifesting to me and all gardeners, the consequences we bring into our lives whenever rebellion raises its ugly head.

It is a humbling experience to work in one's garden. It reveals to us the attitudes of our hearts and the consequences it brings. May we each meditate more on our heart attitudes, as we toil in our garden. It will be beneficial in helping us to learn to exercise our will in a manner which will suppress rebellion, and substitute in its place a sense of humility. God has given an object lesson to assist us in accomplishing that feat. May we utilize it to the fullest.

Praise God for His infinite wisdom!

Father, I am a rebel. I know you know that, but it has to be brought home to me on a daily basis. I thank you for providing gardening difficulties as an object lesson. Continue to reveal to me the attitudes of my heart as I work in my garden. Remove every last rebellious attitude. May humility become a hallmark of my life as a result of being a gardener. I know humility is pleasing to you, and I do so want to please you. Yet, I also know the attitudes lurking just beneath the surface of my heart. May you continue to forgive me when they surface, and bring me back to reality in my garden. In Jesus' name I pray. Amen.

DAY 3
NOTHING IS USELESS

And out of the ground made the Lord God to grow every tree that is pleasant to the sight, and good for food; the tree of life also in the midst of the garden, and the tree of knowledge of good and evil.

And the Lord God said, Behold, the man is become as one of us, to know good and evil: and now, lest he put forth his hand, and take also of the tree of life, and eat, and live for ever: Therefore the Lord God sent him forth from the garden of Eden to till the ground from whence he was taken.

(Genesis 2:9; 3:22-23)

Thought for the day:
Useless things may give us the most profound lesson. Let us listen carefully before we ignore them.

Living in upstate New York a few years ago, I had a difficult gardening problem. The west side of my house received very little sun. This problem was compounded further by it being about six feet from the foot of a terrace. The soil had very poor drainage, and water running off of the terrace would lay on the ground for several days. Nothing would grow along side the house. As a result, the house looked very barren when viewed from the west side.

I was determined to resolve the problem. Looking through the gardening catalogs, I read a blurb on ferns. It seemed like they would be an ideal plant for the location. Besides, I had often seen ferns in the woods and they made an attractive cover. I ordered several plants. When they arrived, they were planted and shortly I had green ferns brightening the spot.

The first year was fine. They ferns satisfied my expectation fully. However, the second year was a different story. Ferns do not like to stay where planted. They send out long roots and the plants come up in places where they are not wanted. Worse yet, where they were planted, they didn't come back. Those ferns turned out to be the most useless plant I ever had in my garden.

One day as I was writing this book, I thought about those useless ferns. During my musings, my mind started to consider the Garden of Eden and the plants therein. Suddenly I realized there was a connection between the ferns and this devotional.

In the Bible, there appears to be another useless plant. It was found in the Garden of Eden. This plant was even given a very special place in the very center of the garden. Attention is even called to the plant by giving it a name, instead of lumping it with all the other plants. It was a tree called the tree of life.

There was absolutely no apparent reason why God should plant the tree of life in the very center of the Garden. Adam and Eve were sinless when first created. Death didn't enter into the world until after their act of disobedience. Therefore, they didn't need to have a tree to give them life. They could have lived eternally without the tree, provided they stayed sinless through obedience. After their rebellion, God drove them out of the Garden so they wouldn't eat of the tree and live forever. Furthermore, God ordered Cherubims and a flaming sword to defend the approach to the tree. The tree was of no use to Adam and Eve prior to the fall, and it couldn't be reached after the fall. The tree of life had no purpose, whatsoever.

Thinking about the worthlessness of the tree of life, it just didn't make any sense. Why would God go to all of the trouble to plant the tree in a very special spot and call our attention to it in His word? God doesn't make worthless things. He most certainly doesn't go to great lengths to call our attention to something of no benefit. Yet, it appeared this was what He had done with the tree of life.

When I get into this type of dilemma, I start to meditate very deeply about the passage, and the context in which the passage appears. There had to be a reason for this useless tree. I had to be overlooking something. As I rolled ideas over and over in my mind, it dawned upon me there were two trees mentioned in the passage. The tree of knowledge of good and evil was also in the center of the garden. All of a sudden, the Holy Spirit opened my eyes to the significance of the two trees standing side by side. They are there to highlight the stupidity of man.

There was only one tree in the garden Adam and Eve were forbidden to eat. The Bible tells us God <u>commanded</u> the man <u>to eat freely of every tree</u> in the garden **except** the tree of knowledge of good and evil. Adam and Eve could have eaten from the tree of life anytime they desired. Had they obeyed God, they would have had eternal life. Instead, they chose to disobey and eat the forbidden fruit. In doing so, they chose death.

Isn't that a stunning example of man's inability to make a sound decision? Why would anyone choose death over life?

However, it goes on every day. People commit suicide, rather than go on living. They take drugs creating a slow death in their bodies, instead of choosing to live a productive, useful life. The worst choice man makes concerns Jesus. Tens of thousands reject him and choose death, when they could have life by accepting His gift of salvation. Modern man is no smarter than Adam and Eve. They consistently choose death over life.

The tree of life and the tree of knowledge of good and evil present a stark contrast. Obedience brings life. Disobedience brings death. One we are commanded to eat of freely. The other is forbidden us. Left to our own means, we still make the same wrong choices as Adam and Eve. Rebellion is at the very center of our lives, just as it was the central issue in the Garden of Eden. Wouldn't it be nice if we could learn something from history? Why don't we?

Those ferns I planted taught me a valuable lesson. Everything the garden catalogs say should be read very carefully. The write up on those ferns told me they were free growing plants that didn't like to stay put. I chose to ignore the warning, because they seemed to give me a solution to a perplexing problem. Instead, over a period of time, they caused me more problems than the original one. Next time, I will be very careful to read and consider the whole write up, not just pick and choose.

The same lesson should be applied to the Bible. When we come to reading it, we should consider the total message. Often, we pick and choose only those passages which do not step on our toes or cause us any distress. We like to think we are okay and doing fine. Later, we may find some plant of sin running wild in our lives.

The Bible calls us to obedience. It has given us a graphic illustration in the Garden of Eden. Let us choose to obey and reap eternal life. Disobedience brings the same result today that it did in the Garden -- death. Let us choose life. May Christ rule in our hearts. Let us obey and make Him our Savior and our King. It will be a choice of life over death.

Father, thank you for the lesson of the tree of life and the tree of knowledge of good and evil. Nothing in your word is useless. May I be ever ready to consider the meaning of all you have written. It is there for my instruction. Obedience to its lesson gives eternal life. May I partake of it and not choose death. When I make the wrong choice, please forgive me and wake me up. Send more useless ferns into my life. They did teach me a valuable lesson. Thank You in Jesus' name.

DAY 4
A QUESTION OF MORALITY

But of the tree of the knowledge of good and evil, thou shalt not eat of it: for in the day that thou eatest thereof thou shalt surely die.

And the serpent said unto the woman, Ye shall not surely die: For God doth know that in the day ye eat thereof, then your eyes shall be opened, and ye shall be as gods, knowing good and evil. (Genesis 2:17; 3:4-5)

Thought for the day:
When the chips are down, where do we look for answers regarding moral decisions? Do we accept God's Word, or do we react according to our human nature?

Yesterday, we took a look at a stunning contrast in the Garden of Eden. We saw God giving us a decision to make between obedience and life, or disobedience and death. Adam and Eve demonstrated the way man would choose down through the ages by choosing the way of death.

Today, we shall look at another startling act of God when He planted the Garden. It centers around a very profound question. "Since God knew the tree of knowledge of good and evil would be detrimental to man, why did He plant it in the Garden in the first place?" Have you ever thought about the reason God performed such a deed? As we look at the answer today, we will see a very important lesson for our lives.

God in His infinite wisdom had given man a mind capable of discovering and analyzing facts. However, there was no guarantee man would utilize his mind in the best way. God, therefore, decided to plant the tree to test man's ability to make decisions in a proper way. He had to see how man would function, so He could have fellowship with man. The test was designed to determine where man would turn when it came to questions of morality. Would they seek God's advice, or would they seek to find out for themselves?

Before we proceed to far, we need to make a fine distinction regarding the word of God. God doesn't forbid knowledge. God wants man to use his mind and gain knowledge. If the Father didn't want us to seek answers regarding life, the universe, our environment, and how things function we would have been forbidden to do so. This He has not done. Our minds are to be used and learning is to take place.

The tree Father planted in the Garden was not the tree of scientific knowledge from which man would have been forbidden to eat. It was the tree of knowledge of good and evil. The fruit of the tree permitted man to decide questions of morality. It did not instill within him empirical, scientific type knowledge. When Satan came to Eve, He didn't tell Eve she would be as smart as God. He told her she would be as the gods, knowing good and evil. The temptation was a question of deciding how one would determine one's morality.

Contrast the tree of life with the tree of knowledge of good and evil. The tree of life would have given man eternal life. All he would have to do is obey God and accept what God had said was bad. He wasn't to question God's judgement on matters of morality. On the other hand, man could disobey God, partake of the tree of knowledge of good and evil. If he did so, man would be responsible for his acts of immorality. We are all well aware of the decision Adam and Eve made.

Let us not be too hasty to condemn that first couple. We all exhibit the same tendencies. When questions of a moral nature arise, where are we most apt to go for an answer? Before we say the Bible, let each of us consider these questions. "Have I ever made a decision to lie?" "Have there been times I have gone back on my word?" "Did I ever seek to deceive someone?" "Are there things I've tried to cover up so I wouldn't be found out?" "Do I always pray and ask God to help me do the right thing?" "Am I totally acquainted with God's requirements in every thing I may do?" "Have I been carrying around bitterness toward someone?"

If we are truly honest, we have to admit our failure to always apply the Word of God to our every action. We do exactly what Adam and Eve did. We decide things for ourselves. Most often it is to our detriment just as it was for Adam and Eve. I had this lesson demonstrated very graphically one summer in my flower garden. Instead of going to an authority, I decided to find out for myself a question about a given plant.

On the east side of my house was a very steep bank. In fact it was so steep it would have been extremely difficult to mow. It made the end of the house look way out of proportion because it made it look extremely high. I decided it should be turned into a rock garden with all sorts of flowering plants to give it an eye catching appeal. It would draw attention away from the house and add beauty to an otherwise drab, uninteresting area. It turned out very successfully.

I like to plant unusual types of plants in my garden. However, during the winter season I usually forget where I planted them. I can never be sure what is coming up where the next spring. One spring I noticed this plant turning green and growing rapidly. I wasn't sure if it was a weed or one of my exotic plants from the year before. I decided it was too much trouble to consult one of my gardening books and check the leaf structure. I would just let it grow a little and then I would be able to tell. This plant grew like no other plant in the garden. It really appreciated all the watering and fertilizing I was giving it. When it got to be about three feet high I decided it had to be a weed. But, I was curious about what type of weed. As summer cooled, it became very evident. I had grown the healthiest goldenrod in all of New York State.

Obviously, I wanted it out of the garden. I pulled, it wouldn't budge. I pulled harder, it still didn't budge. I had to go and get a shovel to get enough leverage to get it out. It had enormous roots spreading throughout my rock garden. I spent over a half hour getting it all out so it wouldn't affect the garden, next year. Failure to consult my books on flowers, cost me a lot of work. (It probably made me the laughing stock of some of my neighbors, even though they were too polite to tell me.) It wasn't one of my better decisions.

Failure to consult a book of authority on morals has the same effect. It causes nothing but problems. All we have to do is view the world around us and the consequences are very evident. Teenage pregnancy, drunkenness, drugs, abortion, lies, cheating, and infidelity abound. Mankind still insists on deciding for itself questions of morality. Adam and Eve did, and it resulted in death. The same results occur today.

God has given us a book of knowledge on morality. It was His solution to man's desire to make moral decisions. We can take it or leave it. Refusal brings death like the tree of knowledge of good and evil. Acceptance brings life like the tree of life. Moral questions must be left to God. Anything less will result in goldenrod growing in the garden of our lives. We cannot trust ourselves to make proper decisions.

Father, thank you for demonstrating again in your Word, the importance of coming to you on questions of morality. Only you can truly decide what is right and what is wrong. I especially thank you for the goldenrod you sent. It taught me a valuable lesson. Coax me to always seek your opinion when it comes to moral questions. In Jesus' name I praise you. Amen.

DAY 5
KEEPING THE GARDEN

And the Lord God took the man, and put him into the garden of Eden to dress it and to keep it.
(Genesis 2:15)

Thought for the day:
Destruction comes from unsuspected directions. We need to be always on the alert in keeping our garden against attack.

When God put man into the garden, He assigned to him two specific tasks: to dress it and to keep it. Man was not to be idle. God knew man needed to be kept active in order to achieve satisfaction out of life. God would provide for Him in every way possible.

We are not told to what extent Adam had to go, in order to cultivate the garden. Since sin had not yet come into the world, there may not have been weeds to pull, bugs to destroy, or fungus to control. However, there would have been the need to garner the crop as it became ripe and develop ways to preserve the food until the next growing cycle. It certainly was not a taxing job which God had assigned to Adam. Rather, it would have given him activity and the opportunity to use his mind and hands in a useful way.

More importantly, was the task of keeping the garden. The Hebrew word translated keep means to put a hedge around or defend the garden. God was well aware of Satan's designs. He knew the evil in his heart and the attempts Satan would make to destroy God's creation. Father knew Adam and the Garden were in danger.

God could have destroyed Satan prior to his enticement of Eve. Since there was such a grave danger to Adam and God's creation, we might think God was rather lax in not taking care of Satan. However, God in His wisdom wanted a race of people capable of withstanding Satan's grand schemes of destruction through their own actions. He wanted man to freely choose the way he would exercise the will God had instilled within him.

An infinite wisdom viewed the whole situation and determined it could be successfully dealt with. God knew He could outsmart Satan over the course of history. There would always be a people willing to surrender to love and grace. He would triumph in the long run, and in doing so, bring great glory to Himself. The Garden would not be off limits to Satan, nor would Satan be destroyed at this time.

Satan was free to do as he pleased. He could wander wherever He wanted. Satan would never be able to accuse God of being unfair and not giving him a chance to prove how untrustworthy was God's greatest creature. Satan must be allowed to prove himself a liar and a destroyer. He would go to his final fate with no alibi, whatsoever.

God, nevertheless, warned Adam of the possibility of danger. He wanted Adam to be on guard and to protect the Garden God had put under his stewardship. History tells us how miserably Adam failed the charge. Satan was allowed into the garden. Eve was enticed, Adam followed her. Satan had established a beachhead from which he could carry out his destructive schemes. Adam did not keep the garden. He let his guard down and destruction took its toll.

My family had just moved back to New York State. We bought a house, and I picked out the spot for the garden. We lived on a terraced hillside. The soil was very poor with hardpan and shale rock just a few inches below the surface. In order to have a productive vegetable garden, I had to build a frame and fill it with topsoil. After completing the bed, I went one step further. I took a very fine wire mesh and nailed it all around the garden. I was not about to allow the rabbits and woodchucks to share in the produce. I was going to do my best to defend my garden from any attack.

The master bedroom in the house was on the second story overlooking the backyard where the garden grew. Every morning on rising, I enjoyed going to the window and looking down on the straight rows full of growing vegetables. One morning I looked down and did a double take. I didn't see my tomato plants. Quickly, I dressed and ran out to the garden to see what the problem was. Each tomato plant had disappeared. I checked the fence thinking a rabbit may have gotten in during the night. The fence was solid. I went back to where the tomato plants had been and there I noticed the unmistakable tracks of a deer.

Destruction entered my garden because I didn't keep it well. Living on the edge of an urban development and very close to a busy four lane highway, I didn't think deer would be a problem. I failed to provide the necessary protection. As a result I paid a price for my laxity.

Adam also paid a terrible price for his laxity. The Garden of Eden would no longer be his home. His labors in obtaining food were compounded. The ground became cursed. Weeds, drought, fungus, excessive rain, poor seed, poor ground would all be part of the struggle Adam and all generations after him would have to face. The penalty for letting down one's defenses is always very severe.

We have been given a charge to keep ourselves from Satan's attacks. Peter tells us Satan is like a roaring lion always on the prowl seeking someone he can devour. He has grand designs on every Christian. Nothing gives him more enjoyment than causing God's people problems. Satan is waiting for just the right moment when our guard is down to make his attack. He is ever watchful. When the time is right, we can be sure he will make his move.

We can not be lax like I was with my garden or Adam was with his. Alertness and extra precaution is always necessary. One brief moment is all it takes for Satan to begin his onslaught.

There are several things we need to do in order to keep our guard in place.

<u>The Bible must be read, studied, and meditated upon.</u> The Word of God is of utmost importance. We need to have personal times of getting into the Word. Each morning needs to see us putting up a fence by making the Bible part of our lives. Additionally, God has given us teachers and pastors to explain the truth of the Word. We must seek out and learn from great teachers.

<u>Prayer is also necessary.</u> We should be looking for God's direction in all things. Weaknesses must be brought to light and strengthened. The hidden things in our heart must be uncovered and cleansed by God's Word and the Holy Spirit. Seeking God's knowledge about our heart will allow us to build a more sturdy fence. We will have a better knowledge of ourselves and be in a better position to fend off Satan.

<u>Fellowship with holy, believing Christians who can pray with us, encourage us, and point out potential dangers is a third part of our defence.</u> The more we separate ourselves from the world, the more we are removed from Satan's arena. We put ourselves in a fort capable of withstanding his attacks. Finding truly committed Christians and making them a part of life is something many Christians fail to see as being necessary. They like to retain their old friends. They feel uncomfortable with real, holy, righteous people. As a result, their lives soon fall prey to the master lion.

I didn't keep my garden well. It was attacked from an unsuspected source. Adam didn't keep his garden well. He too fell prey and suffered loss. May we keep our spiritual garden, our soul, with much greater care.

Father, I was very upset at the deer eating my tomatoes, but I did learn a valuable lesson from it. I praise you for these little difficulties that teach such great eternal lessons. You certainly are the master teacher. Please continue to give me insight on keeping my soul from Satan's attack. Open my eyes and let me see the areas where my fence is not strong. Help me to improve my defenses through your word, your insight, and help from my brothers and sisters in Christ. In Jesus' name. Amen.

DAY 6
BROKEN FENCES NEED REPLACING

How long will ye imagine mischief against a man? Ye shall be slain all of you: as a bowing wall shall ye be, and as a tottering fence. (Psalms 62:3)

Thought for the day:
Fences grow old and need to be kept in repair. Failure to replace established fences can ruin any garden.

My garden fence was unable to keep the deer out of my garden because I did not anticipate an attack from that direction. But, I had made my garden secure against rabbits and woodchucks. For several years, I saw them in the lawn eating the grass, covetously eyeing my vegetables. The fence was strong and secure. The vegetables remained safe from their predatory schemes.

One winter proved to be very harsh. We had heavy snows and winds. By spring time, this combination had bent my fence to the ground. Before I could start my spring planting, I had to put in new stakes and stand the fence up straight. It was starting to rust, and in several places I mended holes. Soon the fence was up and the garden growing nicely.

One spring day, I looked out my bedroom window and was enjoying the beauty of the neat, green rows. There sitting in the middle of the lettuce was a rabbit! Hurriedly, I ran down the stairs, got the hoe, and raced to the garden. I was determined to corner the rabbit in the garden and dispatch him permanently. However, he was able to find the hole by which he had entered and slip out, before I could accomplish my objective. Nevertheless, I found the hole and repaired it. With much satisfaction, I smugly felt the situation was corrected.

Only a few days later, there was a woodchuck in the garden. Again I followed the same procedure. This went on all summer. It was a constant battle against the rodents and repairing the fence. I was able to save most of the crop, but it gave me a lot of anxiety.

God's eternal truths sometimes can only be learned through trials. My bout with the rodents was a trial. However, it did teach me some insights into the word of God. There are two spiritual lessons to be learned from this situation.

The first truth reveals the need to make sure our fences are in good repair at all times. The do grow old and rust. Falling into decay, they allow the enemy to enter, and the enemy can destroy very quickly. If one enters, more will follow and the destruction goes on until the fence is totally repaired.

Our spiritual lives need to be constantly repaired. Virtues we have today, if not continuously kept in good repair, will vanish and no longer stand us in good stead. They need to be constantly inspected and repaired.

Christ came to the apostle John in a vision described in the book of Revelation. During the vision he dictated letters to seven different churches. Basically, these letters dealt with improving and keeping ones virtues in good repair. Two churches were in good repair and Christ encouraged them to keep it so. Five of the churches had allowed their fences to rust.

The church at Ephesus had strayed away from its first love. They no longer had a fervent desire for the things of Christ. Other churches had fallen into various sins. Christ in each case told them He was holding the sins against them. They needed to repent and improve the situation.

It is so easy to allow virtues to slip away. We may start out with a real love for witnessing to others. Some of us may be on fire to show compassion for the homeless and hungry. Others, will have a great desire to study and teach God's Word. Still others, will have the gift of helping others. These virtues are commendable and in need by every church body.

However, through various causes, we tend to lose these talents. Some feel they are over worked and intentionally give up exercising the talents God has given them. Others, will feel unappreciated and begin to turn away. Bodies age and our vitality lessens, so we give up. Slowly, there is an apathy in the church body. It no longer seems to be vibrant, alive, and able to pick us up.

The fence has gaping holes and the enemy enters. People begin to leave the church. Souls are no longer being won to the Lord. Fighting and bickering start to occur among the saints. The church becomes incapable of growing souls.

We need to be on guard. Unless we are looking at ourselves and measuring our lives against the life of Christ, we soon allow the fence to rust and holes to appear. The Christian life must be constantly repaired. Just because we possessed good qualities at one time, is no assurance those qualities are a vital part of our life today. Let us inspect our fences constantly to ensure they will keep the enemy at bay.

Don't let the rabbits and woodchucks have a free meal and destroy the garden God is building in your soul.

The second lesson the fence taught me concerns the proper mending of a fence. When the rabbits and woodchucks got into the garden, I would chase them out, find the hole, and repair it. However, the fence was rusty and old. When the rodents tried to get a meal, they would work their head through and push, The wire would bust and entry was made. The fence needed to be taken down and replaced, not just mended.

Too often, we fail to replace the bad fence in our life. We try to patch it and cover it up. We find out too late, the fence is totally rotten and the enemy can make entry whenever he so desires. Bad fences must be completely changed.

Perhaps we notice some unforgiveness in our soul toward a brother who has harmed us. We know it is wrong, so we resolve to not let it bother us. We go on about our business. Whenever, his action toward us comes to mind, we quickly dismiss it thinking the situation has been resolved. We never really forget about it.

Worse yet, we never take the proper action to resolve the problem. The brother should be approached in a friendly, conciliatory manner and an attempt made to get the matter resolved and true forgiveness attained. The fence is left in a rusty condition.

Failure to completely resolve the problem, may at some later time cause an explosion. This brother may do something else (intentionally or unintentionally). The old resentment is still there and this new incident adds fuel to the fire. We let him have it with both barrels. The enemy has destroyed our witness, and may have destroyed the other brother's walk as well.

The opening verse tells us a tottering fence will lead to our being slain. Satan is out to destroy. If he can get us into situations where we try to patch our fence instead of replacing it, our walk with Christ will shortly be under fierce attack. It might even cause us to become totally slain. Our witness and our life will be of no use to the Master. We fall away from the church and our life becomes a total shamble. May we comprehend the danger.

May our lives be kept in constant review. Let us not allow our fence to rust and the enemy enter. When we do find a rusty fence, may we replace the fence with the proper attitudes. Patching will only delay the inevitable destruction that is sure to follow.

Father, fences around our soul are a vital part of maintaining our relationship with you. Help us to constantly review our fences and find those needing replacement. May we keep our fences from tottering. We thank you for the lesson of the rusty fence. Mighty lessons can be learned from the smallest problems. You are to be greatly praised for communicating such profound truths so very simply. May my fence remain strong. We ask it in the name of Jesus. Amen.

Day 7
LEARN FROM THE WEEDS

> *And unto Adam he said, Because thou hast hearkened unto the voice of thy wife, and hast eaten of the tree, of which I commanded thee, saying, Thou shalt not eat of it: cursed is the ground for thy sake; in sorrow shalt thou eat of it all the days of thy life; Thorns also and thistles shall it bring forth to thee; and thou shalt eat the herb of the field; In the sweat of thy face shalt thou eat bread, till thou return unto the ground;* (Genesis 3:17-19a)

Thought for the day:
Weeds are the most important plants in the garden. They teach necessary and vital lessons about eternal truths.

Weeds are extremely important. Most gardeners, like myself, might at first glance disagree. Certainly, after one has spent several hours on one's knees, while the back stiffened from being in a prone position for so long, one begins to wish there were no weeds. There springs forth an eternal hope of finding a chemical which would only kill weeds and wouldn't touch the flowers or vegetables. Nevertheless, God has provided an extremely important lesson for us in the never ending task of pulling weeds.

When Adam sinned, God immediately cursed the ground. Hence forth it would bring forth thorns and thistles representative of weeds. Man's garden would require many hours of labor to make it productive.

We may think God was being a meany by cursing the ground

for all time. After all, it was Adam and Eve who had sinned. Why should all of mankind have to pay for their evil? The answer lies in looking within ourselves and then viewing God as the master teacher.

When we look at ourselves, we realize we are great sinners and in no more favorite position than Adam and Eve. Adam spoke for the human race and showed God the rebellion, independence, and self-determination qualities which govern all of us. Rather than submitting to God's way, we must find out for ourselves. We need to be constantly reminded of the devastation sin brings into our life.

God the master teacher, seeing our need for a reminder, proceeded to place in our midst a living lesson. Weeds are a destructive force. They can devastate a garden in a relatively short period of time. As we view them, and as we pull them, we ought to be saying to ourselves, "Sin brought this destruction."

One year this lesson was made very clear to me. My flower beds started out very lovely and productive. However, as a result of work and sickness, I was not able to devote the time necessary to keep them weed free. Toward the end of the growing season, things got righted around and I was able to get busy weeding my garden. When I went around to the end of the house to begin the task, I was shocked at the condition of the garden. While it had only been about eight weeks the garden had gone unattended, the weeds had completely taken over. There was not a lot of beauty to be seen. Hours were required to restore the garden to a weed free state. However, the plants had been deprived of the fertilizer they needed to be productive. The beauty for that season was lost.

Life is very much like that flower garden. When sin comes into our life, it can very quickly gain a solid foothold and overrun the good qualities in our life. Without our realizing it, our actions, thoughts, and manner of speech begin to radiate evil, instead of beauty. People will openly see the deteriorating quality of our life. When we come to our senses and turn back to the way of righteousness, the beauty of Christ in our lives has paled. We are not the radiant example of Christ we could have been had the weeds of sin not invaded our garden.

God is such a grand teacher, He actually went beyond giving us one type of weed. He gave us thistles and thorns. This speaks of a variety of weeds. There is a lesson to be learned in this diversity.

Just as thistles and thorns differ from each other and need to be treated in a different way, the weeds in our gardens differ from each other and require different methods of pulling. Some may be pulled very easily. Some need to have their root systems followed beneath the soil so as to get all of it. Some weeds once pulled, are gone for the season. Others require constant work. Some have shallow roots, while others have roots going deep into the soil. These all have applications to weeding out sin in the garden of our soul. God knew exactly what He was doing when He cursed the earth. His lessons are there for our edification, if we are willing to search them out and apply them to our lives.

Job had a sin in his life. The Bible tells us Job was righteous in his own eyes. He took a great deal of pride in his righteousness. This self praise was a danger to his walk and testimony. God allowed Satan to attack Job so the sin could be brought to light.

Job in his last defence before his three friends said, "If my land cry against me, or that the furrows likewise thereof complain; If I have eaten the fruits thereof without money, or have caused the owners thereof to lose their life: Let thistles grow instead of wheat, and cockle instead of barley." (Job 31:38-40a). Job knew sin had brought a curse to the land. He was willing to see the curse applied to his acres, if there could be found sin within himself.

Job didn't know himself very well. There was sin within. Just as Job could not see the sin in his life, we often cannot see the sin in our life. We also do not know ourselves very well.

We may know we are sinners, but we may not know the types of sin existing within. We need to weed our garden very carefully noting the various types of sin God brings to our remembrance. Then we need to seek out the proper way to get rid of the weed. Some of those sins will be shallow. Others will go very deep. Some will be very apparent. Others will be hard to see. Each will require a special type of handling, if the roots are to be totally pulled out.

Weeds destroy our flower and vegetable gardens. The good gardener will be ever alert to the first little seedlings pushing through the soil. They will quickly pull them out, before they can get their roots established.

Sin destroys the garden of our soul. May we be as alert as a gardener, moving quickly to pluck them out lest they take over our lives and get firmly established. When they do, they are much harder to destroy.

Isn't God a great teacher? Aren't you glad He cursed the ground and gave us weeds as a reminder of the destructive quality of sin and the need to apply different methods to get rid of the various sins? God's wisdom is so profound, and yet so easy to comprehend. He speaks to everyone in the simplest ways, yet with a depth of intelligence way beyond anything man can approach.

I praise God for His lessons. Each time I weed my flower and vegetable gardens, I learn a little more about weeding the garden of my soul. We gardeners are truly blessed, when we find weeds among our plants. May we enjoy our weeding and learn from the Master.

Father, I praise you for weeds. They have provided countless hours of labor, but they have also provided lessons of eternal truth. A weed is more than just a noxious plant, it is a gem of wisdom from your infinite wisdom. Instead of complaining about weeds, may I learn from them and apply their teaching to my life. Show me the weeds in my life, and help me to weed the garden of my soul. I would make it a thing of beauty, in order to glorify you. I ask it in the name of Jesus. Amen.

DAY 8
GOD SAW IT ALL

And God said, Let us make man in our image, after our likeness: (Genesis 1:26)

According as he hath chosen us in him before the foundation of the world, that we should be holy and without blame before him in love. (Ephesians 1:4)

Thought for the day:
God planned His creation and foresaw all the problems man would create for Him. He still proceeded, knowing He could overcome all the problems.

I doubt if a non-gardener, or perhaps even a Southern gardener, can appreciate the elation and excitement a Northern gardener feels when the seed catalogs start to arrive. They normally come in late December or early January. The landscape is drab and dreary. Snow covers the land, piling up in drifts and making driving a hazard. Temperatures are in the teens and the wind whistles around the corner. The catalogs arrive and the gardener pulls his chair up to the fireplace and begins to plan his garden for the coming season.

Winter may seem like a bad time to be thinking about gardening. However, spring is just a few weeks away. The anticipation of being able to get outside and get one's hands in the soil provides the motivation to start dreaming. The catalogs are carefully read, and just the right plants and seeds selected. Anticipation builds as one begins to visualize the benefits which will accrue from another growing season.

Along with all the anticipation, there is a realization of the work facing the gardener. There will be earth to till, seeds to sow, plants to set out, fertilizer to spread, weeds to pull, fungi to battle, and crops to be harvested. To realize all the benefits the garden will bring is going to require a lot of hard work. Nevertheless, the gardener presses ahead with his plans. He knows he can overcome the difficulties. Problems cannot destroy the anticipation of what the end result will be.

In the seed catalogs and all the winter planning, I see the reality of a loving God. They demonstrate how God has acted over the eon of time to demonstrate His faithfulness and power toward those who love Him.

Come with me into a time machine. Let us project ourselves back to the time when the stars, planets, and space dust did not exist. Everything was bleak and dreary. There is a total lack of anything, except one thing. The Godhead is present.

We see God sitting down with the other two members of the trinity. They are discussing plans for the creation of the universe. God speaks to Christ and the Holy Spirit about His desire to create a being called man. This creature would possess the qualities of God. He would have emotions, the ability to comprehend facts, and the wisdom to make decisions. Man would be instilled with a soul and spirit which would allow him to experience fellowship with the Trinity. Man would become the crowning achievement of the Master Gardener's creation.

Instantly all three members of the Trinity realize the problems this will create. They foresee the fall, the ravages of sin in individual lives, the destruction of the earth God is going to plant for man. They know man will be incapable of overcoming the rebellion, independence, and self-adulation which controls his every action. There is a realization of the labor involved.

All three members of the Trinity know it will cost them a lot of pain and suffering. Christ understands He will eventually have to take the form of a human being, be rejected, cursed, beaten, and suffer the most agonizing death possible. God feels the pain of having to see his Son bear this torture. The Spirit knows He will have to take up abode in the bodies of sinful, imperfect beings, in order to be their comforter and guide.

It is going to take a lot of hard labor and pain. Still the anticipation of the beauty of a creature in their own image is strong. They look beyond the problems and see the harvest of their labors. They know the difficulties can be overcome and the end result will be a reaping of a garden of souls. The decision is made to press ahead.

Every gardener wishes it could be easier to produce a garden of beauty and utility. We readily accept the toils ahead because we know the enjoyment the garden will bring to ourselves and to others. Fresh vegetables on the table during the summer and stored in the cellar for the supply of our winter needs give us a great deal of satisfaction. The beds and vases of flowers decorating the outside and inside of our homes will add a glow of beauty to their surroundings. We know it will be worthwhile. Nothing will stop us from our tasks.

Can you begin to anticipate the same feelings the Trinity must have had as they planned creation? Seeing all the problems, it could have been very easy for them to turn aside and create a different world entirely. Nevertheless, they knew the value of being able to experience fellowship with a creature having their own likeness. They could foresee the beauty such a creature would cast upon the earth. The effort would be worth it all. They began to create.

Their actions place a great burden upon man. Just as plants are expected to grow and produce else they are destroyed, man also is expected to grow and produce. Some never do. They face an eternity of constant suffering.

Still the garden of God's redemption will produce a bountiful harvest of souls. There will be a Heaven full of individuals with whom God can have fellowship. Their beauty reflecting the image of Christ will grace Heaven's portals. The warmth of love flowing from man toward the Godhead will produce a satisfaction beyond description. Equally true is the love flowing from the Godhead toward their supreme creation --the new creature in Christ Jesus.

Seed catalogs bring a ray of anticipation to every gardener's life. They brighten the dismal landscape at a barren time of the year. Christians need to bring the same glow to a world barren in sin. Our lives, lived in accordance with the Savior's dictates, can produce an immediate brightening, as we await the final harvesting at the end of the age. At that time our lives will have come to full bloom and God's storehouse will be full. The toil will be worth it all. May we press ahead knowing we can overcome any problems which may arise. We have the Master Gardener as a consultant.

Our souls are very valuable plants. They need plenty of care. Nevertheless, if we plant them with the Word of God, fertilize them with daily prayer, and allow the Holy Spirit to water us with His wisdom, the task can be accomplished. We can become an entirely new creature fashioned in the image of Jesus. How bright we will shine in this world of sin and degradation. Our lives will be more productive and the reaping of souls will be greatly increased. Let us allow God to grow our souls.

I appreciate seed catalogs. They bring such a treasure of God's truth. I hope I never lose my zest for gardening. There is so much to be learned.

Father, I thank you for the truth contained in the seed catalogs. I especially am appreciative of the fact you anticipated all the problems and still thought the toil and trouble would be worthwhile. May my life produce a garden of beauty to those around me. May it not only refresh others, may it also strengthen my resolve to live fully in the light of your word. When the final harvest appears, I want to be a part of the reaping. You truly have planned a bountiful harvest and are fully capable of making it happen. Thank you so very much. In the name of Jesus I praise you this day. Amen.

DAY 9
HUMANS ARE FOUR DIMENSIONAL

And when the woman saw that the tree was good for food, and that it was pleasant to the eyes, and a tree to be desired to make one wise, she took of the fruit thereof, and did eat, and gave also unto her husband with her; and he did eat. (Genesis 3:6)

Thought for the day:
Humans have four basic needs. When we see and feed only three, we wander off the path God has designed, and destruction is around the corner.

The devil wanted to wreck havoc. He also wanted to be sure he wouldn't fail in getting Adam and Eve to disobey, so he attacked with all the weapons at his command. We all know the victory he won that day. It was a campaign we should study very carefully for it shows the tactics of the enemy, while pointing out the glaring weaknesses in our defenses.

The first attack Satan made was to the satisfaction of one's physical needs. The apostle John calls it the lust of the flesh, citing it as one of the three points of attack where sin can breach the walls of our fortress. Eve understood the tree was good for food. It was capable of providing real satisfaction to the body. One of her weak points came under attack.

How often we hear people talk about food saying, "It's one of the few enjoyments I get out of life." They say it knowing full well they are overeating and are obese. A heart attack is in the making, but they don't care.

My mother suffered from diabetes. She wasn't supposed to eat sweets, but she went right ahead and had some on almost a daily basis. Just the other day I heard about a man who had suffered a heart attack. He was very overweight, but he still wouldn't cut down. He ended up back in the hospital with another severe attack. These were all "enjoyments in life" by satisfying the flesh.

Other people satisfy the flesh through sex. There is no need to write extensively about the problems this brings into life. It runs the gamut from venereal disease and AIDS through broken homes, fatherless children, and abortion. All so the flesh can be satisfied.

There is no question the desire to satisfy one's flesh is a weak point in our defence. As a perpetual dieter, I can attest to the lure offered by a large prime rib, baked potato with sour cream, and cherry cheesecake. It is difficult to say, "No". Yet, we are expected not to allow the enemy to breach our wall through the desire to satisfy our flesh. Paul calls us to crucify our flesh. If only Eve would have tried harder, she might have resisted the devil.

The second chink in our armor is the satisfaction of our emotional needs. Again, John calls it the lust of the eyes. Eve saw the fruit as pleasant to the eyes. Her emotions were aroused.

Our eyes create emotional needs. All we have to do is ask any retail store manager. They know the power of impulse buying. Have you ever noticed how they always have candy right by the check out lane. They also never have enough lanes manned, so you have to stand in line to spend your money. You keep glancing over at that chocolate. With each glance the desire to give oneself some personal satisfaction becomes a little stronger. Soon our ability to refuse is destroyed and another "little purchase" is made.

Jesus tells us we should pluck out our eye if it is causing us to sin. If we took the injunction literally, there would be a lot of one eyed people walking around. Our eyes allow our inner emotions to be stirred up. We have our desires aroused. Sin is very close to satisfying our weakness.

The third weakness in our defenses is the area of our mind. People have a basic need to know. It fulfills their pride to be able to show how much they know about some given area of life. Eve wanted to be wise. Satan had told here she could be as smart as the gods. It touched her pride. She would know the difference between good and evil. Nobody would have to tell her, "You can do this, but you can't do that". She would be able to decide for herself.

The three areas of life where sin can attack were exposed. Eve's sense of pride through knowledge, satisfaction of emotional needs, and fulfillment of a physical need all came together under one onslaught from Satan. The fall occurred.

However, the fall was not inevitable. Eve didn't have to partake of the apple. Even though all three weaknesses were under attack, she could have resisted. She failed to do so due to her ignorance about her nature. She saw herself as a three dimensional person, instead of a four dimensional one.

In addition to flesh, emotions, and intellect, man has a spiritual dimensional. This fourth dimension can only be satisfied when the other three dimensions are brought into submission. Then the spirit is freed to have communion with God.

With the spirit freed for communion, the Holy Spirit is welcomed into one's life. Christ's in-dwelling manifests itself. His life becomes our life. We dwell hourly in the very presence of God. Life becomes much more complete, for it is exactly what God had planned all along. Had Eve resisted the flesh, her emotions, and her intellectual weaknesses, she and Adam would have remained forever in the Garden of Eden. God would have walked with them in constant communion. Life would have been a life of bliss instead of pain, sorrow, and hard work in order to provide for one's food and the propagation of the human race.

I learned this lesson one day in my garden. My petunias had started out growing vigorously one spring. They had received the three basic needs of all plants: sunshine, water, and fertilizer. They responded by developing quickly and showing the promise of being the best petunias I had ever grown. One day I went out to appreciate my garden and my heart dropped. Several of my best plants were a sickly yellowish-green. Close inspection showed they were under attack by slugs and snails. It was several days before I was able to buy and apply a snail poison. By then I had lost several nice plants.

Satisfying just the three basic areas of those plants development eventually led to their destruction. They had a fourth need -- the protection from outside harm. Ignoring this fourth area proved fatal to the plants.

We humans have the same needs. We need to have our bodies, emotions, and intellect satisfied. Nevertheless, this will never allow us to come to full fruition as a human being. It is only when those needs are satisfied, while under control by our spiritual satisfaction, can we lead a life truly satisfying to ourselves and pleasing to our God.

Ignoring our spiritual need will eventually lead to our destruction, just as surely as it did for my petunias. We need to be protected and saved from outside destruction. The in-dwelling Spirit manifesting the life of Christ provides the necessary protection. May we learn the lesson of the petunias.

Father, I thank you for the insight into our four dimensional needs. May we not ignore the need for personal protection like I ignored the need of my petunias. Eve failed to understand the importance of this fourth dimension. It brought her and her family real problems. Please keep it ever before me. Destroy my petunias again, if it is necessary to wake me up. Father, I appreciate your lessons in life. They have such deep meaning and help your children to understand in a very simple way the pathway of life. I thank you in the name of Jesus. Amen.

DAY 10
WEAK ROOTS ARE HARD TO DESTROY

Brethren, if a man be overtaken in a fault, ye which are spiritual, restore such an one in the spirit of meekness; considering thyself, lest thou also be tempted.

For if a man think himself to be something, when he is nothing he deceiveth himself. (Galatians 6:1, 3)

Faithful are the wounds of a friend;
(Proverbs 27:6a)

Thought for the day:
Some sins appear to be easy to destroy. Still, their roots may continue to linger and begin to grow when we least expect them.

I was weeding my flower beds one day when I noticed a new type of weed. It had a very distinctive leaf and was easily recognizable. I took hold and it pulled out readily. There was no struggle or need to use a weeding tool to get its roots. I could see its short roots hanging down. Confident the weed was destroyed, I tossed it into the weed pail.

Two weeks later, I went back to the bed to check on its condition. There was that weed multiplied several times over, all through my garden. I went after it with a vengeance. As I pulled, I began to notice something. The root wasn't as short as I had originally thought. In fact, it propagated itself by sending out long runners just under the mulch. At varying intervals along the root a new plant sprang up.

In trying to destroy its root system, this weed proved to be very difficult. Its roots were very tender and broke off easily. It was almost impossible to follow the root to its full length. Wherever a piece remained, I knew it meant the plant would be sprouting anew in a few days. I never was able to completely eliminate the weed from the flower bed. The best I could do was to keep it under control by frequent pulling.

As I thought about this weed, I saw a comparison to some types of sin. As a result, I gained a very valuable insight into the struggle we all face in overcoming the sin that so easily besets us. It also taught me something about my relationship with my brothers in Christ.

We sometimes find it very easy to recognize a sin in our lives. God's Word speaks to us very plainly as the Holy Spirit gives us insight into our situation. We know we have to work on the problem. We immediately make a decision to never let the little beast attack us. Over the next few days, weeks, or months we are very careful not to let it ever again manifest itself. We lay aside the attention we have been bestowing upon it, confident we have overcome its influence in our lives.

However, we fail to realize its roots have made their way into our life. It was so easy to dispose of it, we tend to ignore the danger lurking just beneath the surface. Like the weed I pulled in the flower bed, it seems to come out easy. However, its roots are tender and break off leaving a permanent stain in our mind. Given the right situation, it springs to life and grows very rapidly. Suddenly our life is inundated with a major problem.

I tend to think these long, easily breakable roots follow our interaction with others. Three of these weak rooted sins are grumbling, backbiting, and little white lies. We know they are wrong, but in our communications with others, they can so easily sprout we don't even know we have participated until we think about the conversation at a later time. They are part of our human desires and so we are not on guard against them as we should be.

I have often found it easy to grumble and complain when others are doing it. There is something within us that wants to be a part of the crowd. So when they grumble, we grumble right along with them. It really doesn't matter what they are complaining about. It always seems to fit our situation. We just have to join in.

Backbiting is another sin we readily embrace. Someone starts to talk about a person. We suddenly find we have something to add to the conversation. It might be a knowing nod of the head. Other times, it may be comments that really add fuel to the fire. Even though we have been forewarned a hundred times about the evils of gossip, we have never fully pulled its roots out of our lives.

Most of us cannot stand someone telling "bold faced lies." However, most Christians will engage in "little white lies." They do so in order to avoid hurting someone's feelings. We prefer to make up false excuses, rather than tell the truth.

A major problem with this white lie sin, is its tendency to grow. Telling the first little lie causes us to warp our yardstick of truth. The next little lie is measured against an improper standard and ends up being a little bit bigger than was previously possible. Our yardstick warps a little more, and the little lies continue to grow bigger.

Backbiting and grumbling contain much the same danger as the little white lies. Once started, they feed on themselves. Our standards get all bent out of shape. Soon our garden is inundated with all sorts of dangerous weeds. We need a brother or sister in Christ to deal with us and restore us to the righteous walk Christ demands of us.

In order to get better control of these weak rooted sins, we have to take a two pronged approach, just as I did with the weeds in my garden. Anything less, will result in the garden of our soul becoming a very weedy looking mess.

First, we have to try to get as much of the root as possible. The root for these three sins lies in our desire to be accepted. We want to have friends, to participate in fellowship with others. It fulfills a very basic need in our life. Therefore, we are always ready to make ourselves acceptable, and we avoid anything that might be embarrassing. If we are to damage the main root, we have to make a decision to walk with Christ, regardless of what we think might be the immediate outcome. Our relationship with Him will always provide a proper yardstick for controlling our actions.

Second, we have to be on guard against the tendency of these weak rooted sins to sprout anew. Our conversation and dealing with others calls for close scrutiny. Thinking before engaging the tongue will always stand us in good stead.

Have you ever noticed how quick we are to recognize sin in someone else's life? We may even go so far as to get personally involved with the individual, or perhaps, get the pastor to meet with him and tell him what he is doing wrong. However, we should at all times do so with a deep sense of meekness. Lying just beneath the surface is our own little sin ready to make its appearance.

If a brother or sister in Christ comes to us and tries to

inform us of our problem, may we receive it with a readiness to change. Let us not allow ourselves to become totally blinded. They want to help, let them help. That is one of the reasons Christ has created the church. Helping each other to overcome sin will build a stronger body more capable of reflecting Christ.

Weak rooted sins may be quickly recognized and stopped. Nevertheless, they lie just beneath the surface of our desire to be accepted. Let us work at creating a greater desire to be accepted by Christ. It will reduce our need for acceptance by others. We then can begin to really destroy grumbling, backbiting and little white lies. In the end, we will find our acceptance by others has increased and is founded on a much more solid base.

Father, thank you for the lesson of the long, weak rooted weed. I know I needed the lesson, and I am confident others do also. Thank you. Help us to grow in our desire to be accepted by Christ, that we might overcome those sins caused by a desire to be accepted by others. We ask it in Jesus' name and for His glory. Amen.

DAY 11
POCKETS OF SIN REQUIRE TOUGH MEDICINE

But of the cities of these people, which the Lord thy God doth give thee for an inheritance, thou shalt save alive nothing that breatheth: But thou shalt utterly destroy them: ... That they teach you not to do after all their abominations, which they have done unto their gods: so should ye sin against the Lord your God.
(Deuteronomy 20:16-17a, 18)

And they forsook the Lord God of their fathers, which brought them out of the land of Egypt, and followed other gods, of the gods of the people that were round about them, and bowed themselves unto them, and provoked the Lord to anger.
(Judges 2:12)

Thought for the day:
Little pockets of sin provide the breeding grounds for a whole mess of trouble. Left untouched, they will soon start to dominate our lives.

Israel had been forewarned by God to make sure they destroyed every one of the enemy lest they ended up being tempted to follow the enemies' gods. The first chapter of Judges opens with a sad tale of their failure to accomplish the task. Tribe after tribe is listed followed by a comment of how they failed to drive out certain tribes. As a result, they soon became enticed and lured away from the one true God. Judges is a sad commentary on the inability of the nation to follow after Jehovah.

Throughout their history, these little pockets of foreign nationalities caused trouble for the nation of Israel. Over and over again, these non-Israelite tribes would make war and conquer portions of the nation. More subtle was the destruction they wrought through the tendency of Israel to follow their Gods. It eventually resulted in the Israelites being dispersed into foreign countries. It was the only way God could get through to a stubborn and stiff-neck people.

Moving to Florida, I ran into a situation very similar to what the Israelites experienced. I noticed in my lawn a type of weed growing that possessed great destructive powers. It would completely take over a portion of the lawn through its thick growth. The good grass was overrun and eventually died.

When I first noticed this weed it was in small patches around several of the lawn sprinkler spouts. I knew it possessed a danger to my lawn and immediately started to spend hours pulling it out. It proved very difficult to get every last plant. After working a spot over very carefully, I had removed most of the visible weeds. However, some still remained. Furthermore, I knew there were undetected roots still in the ground. I resolved to pay close attention to these areas and keep the remaining weed under control by frequent weeding.

Unfortunately for me, there were too many little spots to weed. By the time I got through all of them, the first ones had sprouted anew, and had actually spread further into the lawn. After two years of futile effort, I have decided the only way to restore my lawn to some degree of beauty is by killing all the grass in the area with a strong herbicide, and then re-sodding it with good grass.

The good grass has suffered badly at the growth of this weed. It is going to take tough action to rectify the situation.

In the end, I will succeed, but it has cost me a lot of time and heavy expense. I learned too late about the danger this weed truly represented. If only I had attacked it with herbicide and replanted small areas in the beginning, I could have saved both time and money. Sometimes we learn slowly.

This incident with the lawn weed, reminded me about the problems the Israelites had with their pockets of aliens. They suffered terribly as a consequence of the evil existing in their midst. In the end, God had to completely drive them out so He could replant them, after their tendency to follow other gods has been destroyed. Eventually, God will bring them to the point of being the type of nation He wants. It requires tough medicine to drive out a tough enemy. The Israelites learned too late the potency of the danger they faced.

These two examples speak to me about the power of sin in our life. Even a little sin left in the deep recesses of our desires, will eventually start to take over our life. Only when it is all purged, can we live in a glorious fellowship with God and our fellow man. It takes a good deal of effort to even begin to approach a sinful nature. It is never accomplished overnight. We must expend time and effort.

Unfortunately, we tend to learn very slowly the importance of overcoming all sin in our life. Each of us have little pockets we don't bother with, either due to our enjoying them, or not thinking they are dangerous to us. It is to our dismay, when we find out they have grown and started to dominate our lives in various ways.

These little sins are as dangerous as the aliens were to the nation Israel. May they not result in our having to be driven out of the fellowship of the church in order to awaken us. Let us be aware of their powerful potential.

I find two situations very heart rendering. One is the Christian who starts out serving the Lord and ends up back into the world living a life of blatant sin. Second is the person who has been a Christian for a good portion of their life and still has a great number of sins they are refusing to drive out. Both types suffer greatly from their inability to rise up against their enemy. Both bring a great deal of harm to the church and to the cause of Christ. My heart breaks over their lack of desire to serve the living God. They are modern day examples of the old nation of Israel. God's people sure learn slowly.

This spring will find me out in the lawn applying the necessary chemicals to destroy a very dominating weed. Six weeks later, I will re-sod the lawn. Hopefully, it will permanently solve the problem. However, should the weed reoccur, I will quickly attack it with all the power at my command. It will never again have the ability to dominate my lawn the way it presently does.

May all of us exercise the same resolve toward the sin in our life. Let us attack it with all the forces at hand. We cannot afford to let it dominate our lives. We also, cannot even allow it to remain in little hidden pockets of our desires. Lurking there it will only toughen and spread its roots. Soon it will start to grow little plants of sin. They will quickly spread to other areas. Let us apply tough medicine early on, before we have to suffer as the Israelites of old suffered. May we learn from their example and from the example of the lawn weed. It will stand us in good stead.

The Old Testament, with its illustrations, and the flora of our earth provide very powerful lessons. God has been so good to give us such clear instruction. It should make us even more appreciative of all He has done on our behalf. God obviously thinks it important for us to understand the need to destroy the weeds of sin. He has given sufficient testimony for our edification. May we be doers of the Word, and not hearers only.

Father: Thank you again for such a clear lesson from your earthly garden. It graphically illustrates the problems we face as we try to grow into the likeness You desire. Please continue to give us these lessons, that we might be better fortified in our determination to drive out any pockets of trouble. We do not, and cannot afford the risk of being dominated anew by sin left in our lives. Call these areas to mind. Give us the resolve to overcome them. Provide the right ingredients to allow us to accomplish the task. We ask it in Jesus' name. Amen.

DAY 12
WEEDING SHOULD BE CONTAGIOUS

Train up a child in the way he should go: and when he is old, he will not depart from it. (Proverbs 22:6)

For even hereunto were ye called: because Christ also suffered for us, leaving us an example, that ye should follow his steps:... should live unto righteousness:
(I Peter 2:21, 24a)

Furthermore then we beseech you, the brethren, and exhort you by the Lord Jesus, that as ye have received of us how ye ought to walk and to please God, so ye would abound more and more.
(I Thessalonians 4:1)

Thought for the day:
The example we set may not be readily apparent. Nevertheless, over time it will take affect, and the gardens of sin in the lives of others will be weeded.

With several flower beds, a large vegetable garden, a yard to maintain, and housework to keep up due to the ill health of my wife, I looked to my teenage son Greg for assistance. He willing responded, and fulfilled whatever was required of him in an excellent manner. However, there was one exception. Greg would not help me pull weeds. As he would put it, "I don't do weeds, Dad." As a result I pulled a lot of weeds while he was doing some other job, and on a rare occasion as he watched. There was no way I could entice him into pulling weeds.

Greg after graduating with his master's degree took a job some distance from us. He rented his first apartment and moved in. One day, as we were talking on the phone, he stunned me with the following remark: "Guess what I did today? I weeded and trimmed the hedge in front of my apartment. It looked so bad, I couldn't stand it. I even took out a pair of old shears and trimmed the bushes."

I rejoiced. A child had been raised up in the way he should go. My good example at keeping the gardens weed free had made an impression. Even though as a teenager, Greg didn't do weeds, he had learned its importance, and as an adult demonstrated how well the lesson had sunk in.

Peter makes a very strong argument for living a life of righteousness by citing how Christ had suffered for us as an example. Jesus lived a totally righteous, holy life; yet in the end, He was treated like a common criminal. According to Peter, we should live to the same degree of holiness, even if the end result is the same as that received by the Lord Jesus. Peter would not have us compromise our principles in order to avoid suffering and persecution. Jesus was the example. We are to walk in His steps. Anything less would be falling short of the mark, hence it would be sin.

I don't know about you, but I find there have been times in my life when I have failed to take a stand, or bent the rules, in order to avoid being made a laughing stock. I certainly have come short of the mark. Afterward, there has been a twinge of conscience calling me to repent and ask for forgiveness. Just as my weeding had made an impression on Greg, which finally manifested itself in his adult years, Christ also had made an impact, even though it was not immediately manifested. How important it is to have an example to follow!

God in His infinite wisdom, desires a second example within His church. In addition to the Suffering Savior, He expects there will be members in each local body of believers, capable of demonstrating a life of righteousness regardless of the cost to them personally. There should be those walking in a manner as to represent to the young, immature Christians, how they are to live life. The Savior then becomes a living example through the life of the mature Christian. It is God's way of training up a child. Examples need to be set so they may be followed by the new babes in Christ. Natural parents know they need to set examples for their children. Spiritual parents have no less an obligation.

However, let us never assume someone else will become that living example. It is the duty of every Christian to become a living example, a spiritual parent. As we read the letters of the apostles, and especially of Paul, we find they continually set themselves forward as living examples. This was not an act of boasting on their part. Rather, it was an admission of how much they had sold themselves out to Christ. They were willingly putting aside all of their personal desires, in order to please Christ. It was their hope and prayer for each Christian to attain to the same level of surrender.

How often we tend to forget our responsibility to the other members of the congregation. We begin to think, if we go to Church on Sunday, attend Wednesday night prayer meeting and go to certain church social functions, we have served the church. In the process, we may very well have fulfilled what the Church expects of us.

However, we will have not fulfilled what Christ expects from us. His standard of service is living a life in conformity to His example. His footsteps are the imprints where our feet are to trod. When we begin to understand the standard Christ sets before us, we will have to take stock of our lives. Undoubtedly, there will be some weeding awaiting us in order to adjust to His call.

Let us ask ourselves the question, "Are there examples of Christ in the congregation where we worship?" If there isn't, we are being cheated. The only example available is limited to our ability to understand what Christ was like as we read our Bibles. We are missing the living example. Now, I do not want to disparage the Word of God. The Bible is extremely important in teaching us about Christ. However, it can become much more real, when we see its message being manifested in the lives of other Christians. It becomes more than a book of words, it becomes a meaningful living example.

Every Christian has been given the responsibility of becoming a living example of the weed free life of Christ. We are to become examples to God's new children so they too can grow in righteousness, eventually passing on the example to a generation yet to come. It is a heavy responsibility we bear.

I am sure there isn't a gardener alive who wants to pass on to the next generation a garden so full of weeds, the flowers can't be seen. Neither should we want to pass on to the next generation, a life so full of the weeds of sin Christ cannot be seen. Our flower bed of righteousness requires us to start weeding immediately.

We may not like "to do righteousness" any more than Greg liked to do weeds. It doesn't fit into our desires. Nevertheless, if Christ has become real to us, there will be a change occurring in our lives. The ugliness of sin gradually becomes apparent. We know some weeding and pruning will improve our overall appearance. Eventually, we are convicted and begin to pull the weeds of sin. Through a steady application of sin pulling, our lives take on the life of Christ. We then end up becoming a living example to the new generation of Christians.

Needless to say, a weed free life will require hours of work. Some will stand by and watch, just as Greg would watch my weeding. This should not cause us any consternation. The lesson is sinking in, even though it is not readily visible.

In time this new generation will pull their own weeds and trim their own hedges. We have raised up a child in the way he should walk, and he won't depart from it. Our hearts rejoice at having passed on a good example.

Father, we love you and thank you for the example you gave us in your Son. May we live our lives as a reflection of His life and pass on to the next generation, a garden of righteousness. Even when we do not want "to do righteousness", convict us strongly so we will move ahead and not sin against you. Our desire is to please you, even when the flesh is weak. In Jesus' name we ask this. Amen.

DAY 13
GOOD PLANTS NEED PRUNING

Every branch in me that beareth not fruit he taketh away: and every branch that beareth fruit, he purgeth it, that it may bring forth more fruit. (John 15:2)

Thought for the day:
Plants that produce abundantly can be made to increase their yield through pruning. God, likewise, increases the fruitfulness of our lives by carefully pruning away those branches which hinder the growth of more fruit.

As I look back over my spiritual life, it seems like I have gone through a continuous cycle of mountaintop highs to desert lows. Things will go very well for a period of time. Prayers get answered, Sunday schools lessons touch people's hearts, the fellowship is warm, sermons touch my heart, and the ever dwelling presence of the Holy Spirit is felt on a daily basis. From there, in almost a flash, it seems like I am in a desert. Prayers don't seem to reach the ceiling, Sunday school lessons lack vitality, fellowship is missing, sermons are dead, and God seems to be light years away. It is the most unpleasant of times. They seem like they will never end, but eventually they do and a new mountaintop high is felt.

As I write these words, Loretta and I have been going through a prolonged desert experience. Over two years ago we moved to Florida and started looking for a church. The area we settled is heavily churched. We have visited numerous churches and still have not found one where we feel we can truly worship and serve. After a while we began to question ourselves. What is wrong with us? Why can't we find what we're looking for? The questions tend to put us in a mood of self-condemnation.

Is there something wrong with us? Are we being too critical of the churches? I believe the answer is negative for both questions. I could start to believe we are missing something, or there is something wrong with us, if I didn't know and believe Scripture. God is just doing a work in our lives. He has to teach us something, so he has created a desert experience for us. It is part of God's plan. He never leaves anything in a finished condition. As the verse for today points out, God is always trying to increase the fruitfulness of our lives. Sometimes, it takes extensive pruning to accomplish the task.

Consider some of the great heroes of the Bible and the deserts God put them through, before He was able to use them in some mighty way. They had to go through extensive periods of training and preparation. It was not a pleasant time for them.

Joseph had to become a slave and then a prisoner, before he could become a ruler in Egypt. The end result of his service resulted in the Jewish nation, as it existed at that time, moving to Egypt where they could grow into a mighty nation. The had peace, food, and protection for four hundred years, while they developed into a large multitude.

Moses went from a reed basket cast adrift in a body of water to living in a palace. From the mountain of the palace, he was thrust into the real training ground of the desert where he herded sheep for forty years. Only then, was he prepared to become the ruler capable of leading the Israelites out of Egypt and through the desert for forty years.

Elijah, after confronting King Ahab and pronouncing God's judgement upon the nation Israel, was directed by God into the wilderness. There he was fed carrion brought by ravens and drank from warm, stagnant pools of water from a creek that was drying up and from which animals also drank. From there he was directed to a foreign land and lived with a widow woman, until God saw it was time for him to come forth and do battle with the prophets of Baal.

David went from serving in Saul's palace to living on the run in the wilderness, being hunted like some wild animal by King Saul. Later, David found himself living in a foreign land among the Philistines, even trying to assist them in war against his own people. Gradually, God pruned away the attitudes He knew would prevent David from becoming a good king. When the proper growth had occurred, David ascended to the throne and had a very successful reign.

Job is another prime example of the pruning God performs. A righteous man who really loved God, he had one little sin in his life. He was self-righteous. Job had to lose everything, as God prepared him for even greater riches and honor. In the end, he became a source of encouragement for God's people down through the ages.

The apostle Paul performed some of his greatest duties for the church while sitting in a jail in Rome. From there he wrote the letters which make up a substantial portion of the New Testament. God, during Paul's life, had pared away all excess baggage, thoroughly preparing him for writing the Scripture needed by the church down through the ages.

The list could go on. God usually takes individuals to the desert prior to taking them up the mountain. He has to bring us low to wring out every bit of pride and self-capability, in order to get us in a position to accomplish His designs. God, the master pruner, knows exactly what is needed and will cut away the right parts. It never is pleasant, but it always is perfect.

I planted a lilac bush on the southeast corner of my house. It was a beautiful bush and the location was perfect for its growth. It produced a fair crop of blooms in the spring. We enjoy the smell of lilac so much we put several branches in a vase in our family room in order to fill the room with its fragrance. We enjoyed the fragrance and beauty for two weeks.

After the blooms were over, I went out and cut off every dead bloom. In addition, I trimmed the branches failing to produce. My neighbors may have thought me crazy for it took me over an hour to properly trim out all the dead blooms and shape the branches. Then, I fertilized it well. The plant grew mightily through the summer and almost doubled in size. The next spring, my neighbors appreciated the benefits of my labors. The bush was abundantly covered with the biggest most fragrant blooms imaginable. The pruning had increased the yield ten fold.

God's pruning accomplishes the same effect. When God has seen fit to use us in some way, He prepares the bush to produce the necessary fruit. As He trims, He sees beyond the present hurt and suffering knowing the results the next mountaintop will produce. The next season will see a bountiful harvest. Rather than despair as we go through these desert experiences, we should rejoice!

If you are going through a desert experience at the

present time, let me assure you it will come to an end. God is an expert in the pruning of lives. He will accomplish the task and bring you out of the desert. Instead of letting gloom and despair settle into your life, begin to anticipate what the next mountaintop is going to produce. The anticipation will drive away the doubts and make the experience an exciting adventure with God.

Learn a lesson from the lilac bush. Even though it produced blooms, the next year proved to be even better. The pruning accomplished an abundant yield. Our lives, pruned by God, will produce the same result. He has given us a lesson in nature, so we will not despair during our wandering through the desert.

Father, thank you for the lesson from the lilac bush. I appreciate how simple and clear you make your lessons. A little bush with some flowers can turn into the mightiest of truth when it is viewed in the light of your word. Continue to prune our lives. We are excited and full of anticipation at what the next season will bring. We are looking for an abundant harvest, because you are the master pruner. May we always be thankful for your work in our lives. Make our garden fruitful. We ask it in Jesus' name. Amen.

DAY 14
RADICAL TREATMENT BRINGS HOPE

Ye have not yet resisted unto blood, striving against sin.
(Hebrews 12:4)

Wherefore lift up the hands which hang down, and the feeble knees; And make straight paths for your feet, lest that which is lame be turned out of the way; but let it rather be healed. (Hebrew 12:12-13)

Thought for the day:
Valuable bushes may need to be cut down when disease hits. However, they have a will to live and will spring forth in new growth. All is not lost. Hope is eternal.

When we lived in Pennsylvania, I had an ideal spot to plant roses. It was on the south end of the house well protected from the cold north winds. I dug a bed the full width of the house and set out climbing American Beauty roses. Then I made a lattice work out of wires strung diagonally from the eaves to posts in the ground. The roses were fed periodically with the proper rose food and watered during dry periods. Rapidly they grew.

By the second summer, the whole side of the house was covered with these rose bushes. Birds even made their nests in their tangled branches. Late in June, they burst forth in masses of bright red blooms. They were a stunning sight and one of my most successful garden ventures. Cars would stop on the street and take pictures of the mass of blooms.

After they were done blooming, I cut off all the dead blooms, and trimmed out unnecessary growth. The following year saw a repeat of the prior summer. They may have even bloomed more profusely. Again, I repeated the process of pruning, fertilizing and watering. I had a good thing going, and I was doing every thing in my power to assure its continued success.

However, the following summer I noticed some leaves turning yellow with black spots. I delayed doing anything for a period of time not being too sure if it was some type of disease, or if it was just a few leaves dying prematurely. The disease started to spread rapidly. By the time I started dusting the plants against yellow leaf and black spot, the bushes were badly affected. I was unable to control the spread. The next spring brought evidence of the devastation. Most of the main shoots were dead and failed to sprout any leaves. There was only one thing left. Cut the bushes down and hope they would spring new shoots from the roots.

My heart ached as I cut each bush to the ground. I was convinced the beauty of the previous years was lost. I could see myself having to start all over with new plants. Much to my surprise, one day I noticed new shoots starting to spring forth from the roots. Quickly, fertilizer and water were applied. Periodically, they were dusted with a good fungicide. The next year the roses were back. The birds once again nested in their boughs. Friends, neighbors, and I were able to enjoy their beauty anew.

The incident with the roses taught me three very valuable lessons about the Word of God. Those lessons were to stand me in good stead as I grew and matured in my understanding of the Bible and the way God operates in a person's life.

The first lesson concerned the rapidity with which we are to act. Yellow leaf and black spot had attacked my plants. I delayed treatment not being certain about the problem. It gave the disease a chance to take hold and ruin good bushes. Had I reacted quickly, I know the bushes could have been spared the radical treatment of having to be cut down. I would have been spared much anguish over their condition.

The same lesson can be applied to situations in our life. Sometimes things start to creep into our life and we may not be sure if it is keeping with the Word of God. We delay dealing with the situation, since we're not sure of its nature. Gradually, we begin to recognize it gaining a foothold and causing other problems. Finally, we decide to act. By then, it may be too late. That particular situation may have become a severe problem. It becomes very difficult to solve.

A good rule is to act first and question later. If we have doubts whether something is proper or not, it probably isn't. We should start treatment right away and destroy the problem before it gains a foothold. Later, if we decide it wasn't a danger, and it can be brought into our lives for a good purpose, we can always institute it. It is much better to deal with minor problems before they become gigantic ones.

One area where this could be effectively applied concerns our relationships with Christian brothers. Any disagreement should be dealt with immediately. Later, if it becomes necessary to take a firm stand against a brother, we can always "stand up and be counted". Normally that will not occur, and our prior actions will have maintained peace in the brotherhood.

The second lesson the roses taught me concerned the type of treatment required. I had to practically destroy the bushes in order to restore them to health. It wasn't until they were totally cut-down and allowed to spring forth with new shoots could they grow and develop the beautiful flowers expected of them. Radical treatment eventually produced beautiful blooms.

God may have to deal with us in the same way. Sometimes we get so caught up in sin, they only way it can be destroyed is by bringing us to the ground. The treatment isn't pleasant, but it has a good motive -- the restoration of lost blooms.

Paul wrote a letter to the Corinth church regarding a particular hideous sin in their midst. He stated the individual should be turned over to Satan for the destruction of his flesh in the hopes his spirit could be saved. This was in keeping with a pattern established by God in the Old Testament. He had to destroy the nation Israel, sending them as slaves to foreign lands in order to destroy their sin of idolatry. It was necessary, if they were ever to bloom again. God sometimes must act in a radical manner toward us, if we are ever to bloom as a Christian.

The third lesson was derived from the new shoots. When things appear totally hopeless, they never are. The plants weren't dead. Their roots were alive. As a result, they were able to once again produce beauty for others.

We may be totally cut down for some reason. Maybe it was because of sin. Perhaps, due to God wanting to prepare us for even greater service. It might be the result of Satanic attack. Regardless of the cause, we should never give up hope.

If plants can grow after they have been destroyed, our souls can certainly bloom anew. We have the power of God dwelling within us. That gives us an infinitely greater chance of growing, than my roses ever possessed. Don't give up hope. Look to the root -- the God of all Creation who can make all things new. He originally created all, hence He can re-create it. Hopelessness is a word that doesn't exist. There is always hope.

Eventually we had to move from Pennsylvania leaving my roses bushes behind. I hope the buyer of the house appreciated their beauty as much as I did. However, I took with me something much more valuable than the memory of their blooms. I had received some valuable insight into God's dealing with us through a very practical lesson from God's creation. We gardeners are such a fortunate lot. God can teach us so much through such mundane things as yellow leaf affecting rose bushes.

Father: I thank thee for the hope we see in the ability of plants to grow again even when they have been destroyed. It is a valuable lesson. May we never forget it. Equally important are the lessons of quick action to ward off potential problems, and the fact we sometimes must be brought low in order to be made to re-bloom. May we always react quickly to any sin in our life so you will not have to bring us down. Thank you for the lesson from the rose bushes. I praise you in Jesus' name. Amen.

DAY 15
LEGAL BUT NOT PROFITABLE

I know not: Am I my brother's keeper?
(Genesis 4:9b)

All things are lawful unto me, but all things are not expedient: all things are lawful for me, but I will not be brought under the power of any.
(I Corinthians 6:12)

Thought for the day:
Our Christian growth is measured by how well we fulfill our responsibilities to our brothers and sisters in Christ — not by the legality of our action.

Growing up on a small farm, instilled within me a deep appreciation for the things God has provided for us. We were very self sufficient utilizing the various fruits God provided in the fields and forest.

At an early age, my mother took my younger sister and me foraging for wild strawberries. We would walk along the shoulder of the dirt road running along side of the house, follow the fences around our fields, and carefully search the pasture for the harvest. These would be picked by their long stem, taken back to the house, and detached. After careful washing and sorting they went into the pot and were made into wild strawberry jam. Usually, some were covered with sugar and set aside in a container. Mom then baked a white loaf cake, and made whipped cream from the milk we had skimmed from our one cow. That night we feasted on huge bowls of shortcake.

    Having learned very young how to find wild strawberries, my sister and I loved to wander into the meadows in search of the fruit. Since the strawberries were ripening at a time when the grass was quite tall, we were told not to go into the meadows, lest we trample down the grass and make it hard to mow for hay. We worked out a way we thought would let us get away with these adventures into the fields. We would get down on our hands and knees and crawl into the grass. Since the grass would be higher than our backs, we assumed nobody would see us. We never guessed our parents were tall enough to see over the grass, and we ventured forth often in search of this delectable fruit.

    Even if we escaped the watchful eye of Mom, she always knew when we had been eating strawberries. Our lips would be stained red. Unfortunately, there was even a more sure sign. I would break out in a rash. I was allergic to strawberries and would get the hives if I ate a lot of them. I would start to cry from the itching. Mom would make a paste of water and corn starch and cover the red splotches. After a few hours, I would be back to normal. A few days later, the pain of the itching forgotten, sis and I would venture forth again. Fortunately, as I grew older, the allergy went away and I now can eat strawberries to my heart's content. However, I still yearn for those wild strawberries from God's garden.

    There is an old adage that says, "What goes around will come around." In the case of the strawberries, this has come true in a somewhat oblique fashion. My wife, Loretta, loves strawberries and always makes sure I plant a bed. I normally have about a hundred ever-bearing plants growing. We freeze some and eat most of them. However, Loretta is allergic to strawberries. On occasion she will break out in huge welts and start to itch. She will suffer for a few hours until the hives disappear. Nevertheless, she still keeps eating strawberries. She hasn't learned to avoid them, any better than I did when I was a kid. They are so good, the pain is worth it.

I relate that story, since it illustrates a point Paul was making in his letter to the Corinthians in the passage cited above. The church in Corinth had a lot of problems. Several of them were eating food previously sacrificed to idols, suing Christian brothers in court, and committing acts of sexual immorality. There was a group within the church with a very liberal attitude toward sin. They took the position, "We are under grace, so we don't have to worry about keeping any laws."

Paul was writing to contradict that attitude. He was quoting their position when he wrote, "All things are lawful unto me." We can be absolutely sure this was not Paul's attitude. He wrote too many letters setting forth things considered to be sin and of the world, urging His readers to stay clear of them, lest they should fall from grace. Paul takes their argument and turns it back upon them. He says, "They may be legal, but that doesn't make them expedient" (better translated profitable).

The Christian life has a different standard than either of two popular religious concepts. The first concept is the Corinthian attitude of disregard for the law, since we are under grace. The second concept is the attitude of the Pharisees and scribes which insists on keeping a detailed list of rules in order to assure our salvation. Both of those concepts are against the standard established by the Bible.

The Holy Spirit saw fit to record Cain's reply to God, when he answered, "Am I my brother's keeper?" As the later giving of the law, and its enlightenment by the prophets and the New Testament writers proved, God expects us to be our brother's keeper. It is exactly that point Paul makes in replying to the Corinthians.

There are many activities we Christians can engage in which may be perfectly legal and not considered sin. For example, there is nothing legally wrong with suing a person who has caused us a financial loss in some manner. We certainly have every right under our legal system to redress that wrong.

The eating of meat previously sacrificed to idols didn't mean the person was worshipping idols. He was only eating food that was readily available to him without any intent of worshipping idols. His conscience was clear and he was acting accordingly.

However, Paul says these things were not proper actions for a Christian. We are our brother's keeper and we need to measure our actions against the standard of how our actions affect them. It is a much greater standard than a mere keeping of the law. It imposes a responsibility to carefully consider every action in the light of its effect upon others.

In the case of suing a brother, Paul says it should not occur in the public arena. The church should handle the matter. Christians shouldn't wash their dirty linen in the public, and thereby bring unnecessary shame to a brother or sister in Christ.

In the case of eating meat sacrificed to idols, there were Christians who wanted to avoid even the appearance of indirectly worshipping idols. To see a brother eating sacrificial meat, bothered their conscience and caused them mental anguish. Paul told the eaters to stop, if there was a brother present who was bothered by their action.

In the same letter, Paul reacted very harshly against those engaged in sexual immorality. Paul called upon the church to judge them and deal with them accordingly. Sin is sin and must be properly judged. There are a lot of actions the Bible definitely says are wrong. We are expected to keep those laws, even if we are under grace. Grace cannot be cheapened by total disobedience to the laws of God. Cheapened grace is grace rejected.

The real test of Christian growth, however, is not how well we keep the law. Rather, it is how sensitive we have become to the condition of our brethren in Christ. We are our brother's keeper. We need to measure our actions against that standard.

Strawberries were food, delicious and proper to eat. They weren't always in our best interest. The hives let us know we had exceeded the bounds of what our body could tolerate. May our conscience let us know when we exceed the bounds of what offends others. It may be legal, but it may not be profitable for us.

Father, thank you for the lesson from the strawberries. Even when I was a child and didn't know You, You were providing instruction which would later mean something, as I came in contact with your Word. Please make my conscience sensitive to the needs of others. Thank you for taking away my strawberry allergy. I sure do enjoy them. I praise you in Jesus' name. Amen.

DAY 16
WEED SEEDS DON'T MIX WELL

But I have said unto you, Ye shall inherit their land, and I will give it unto you to possess it, a land that floweth with milk and honey: I am the Lord your God, which have separated you from other people.
(Leviticus 20:24)

Wherefore come out from among them, and be separate, saith the Lord, and touch not the unclean thing: and I will receive you, And will be a Father unto you, and ye shall be my sons and daughters, saith the Lord Almighty.
(II Corinthians 6:17-18)

Thought for the day:
Good mulch requires a distinction to be made about the material going into it. Individuals and the church need to be careful to separate from the bad, in order to ensure adequate growth and preservation of the truth of the Gospel.

Both in the Old and New Testaments, we find God telling His people they are a separated people. We have been separated from the people of the world, and we are expected to walk accordingly. It is a wondrous thing the Lord has done, yet, so few of us appreciate the mighty necessity behind this important call.

I think I was very fortunate having been born into a family where one parent was an immigrant. It gave me a broadening experience I doubt I would have experienced had I not been so fortunate. Dad came to this country from Germany in 1929. Other than a sister, brother-in-law, nephew, and a couple of friends, he was completely separated from his homeland. He worked hard, learned the language, met an American girl, married, and had a family. He became a good American. American sports, food, freedom, and the rights of citizenship became his. He never went back to Germany, although he did correspond with family.

Even though he was an American in all aspects, I noticed one thing which helped to give me insight into another world. Whenever, Dad would get together with his sister and her husband, He quickly became a German. He spoke their language, played their games, and ate their food. He never truly became separated from his background. He could be a good American citizen, but his German roots were strong and easily called him back.

His experience, unfortunately can be our experience, if we fail to make a complete break from our old way of life. We very easily slip back into old ways. Instead of being a citizen of heaven, we often find ourselves citizens of two countries -- one where we dwell, the other where our roots lie.

God has done His part in separating us from the kingdom of Satan. He has given us the responsibility to walk in a way that will allow us to maintain the separation. We cannot afford to dwell in two worlds. The tendency will always be to go back to our roots. The end result will be disastrous.

Perhaps the best example available to us in the Bible is the record of Lot's wife. I used to think God had treated her very unfairly. The penalty she received seemed to be totally out of line for such a minor disobedience. After all, what harm did she really do by looking back at the destruction of Sodom and Gomorrah? True, she had been commanded not to do so, but her disobedience didn't affect the destruction of the city, or anyone else. Why was she penalized so severely?

We Christians tend to be more disobedient than she was. We often ignore God's Word in ways that are more disruptive to God and to our fellow man. We fight with each other, fail to feed, house, and clothe those in need. Our love and compassion can be non-existent at times. Compared to Lot's wife, our sin appears to be much more destructive. Yet, we do not suffer the penalty she suffered.

The reason, of course, lies in her attitude. She was not separated from the world. Her heart was still back in Sodom. Even though she may not have openly participated in the sins of those two cities, she must have enjoyed the avant-garde life style all around her. The filth surrounding her gave her a certain amount of pleasure. When she was separated from the city by God, her heart still remained with the sins of the city. Looking back, she represented to God her longing for those sins. God realized, she had not allowed herself to become separated. Her heart was back with her roots. He had no other choice. She had to be destroyed for the sake of Lot and her daughters.

God has done His part. Just as God separated Lot's wife from the world by calling her to come out of the world of sin, God, through His Son, and call, has separated us from the world. It is up to us to signify to Him, the completeness of our separation. Something Lot's wife failed to do.

There are two ways we are to become separated from the Kingdom of Darkness.

First, we should begin to associate with new friends. Rather, than participating in activities with our old relationships, we should separate ourselves unto new activities with other Christians. Time spent fellowshipping with them, strengthens our resolve to grow in Christ. We learn how to pray, study the Bible, and walk in faith. God sees the desires of our heart, and through His Holy Spirit provides the power to grow in the grace and knowledge of the Lord Jesus. We rapidly become mature citizens of a new country.

Second, and equally important, we need to be careful about the people we allow to become a part of our membership. Our churches need to be open to all people. The sinner has to hear the Gospel and come to a saving knowledge of Christ. However, to take part in the decisions of the church requires a people that is truly born again and walking by the Spirit. They will make sure the church retains its distinct character of a holy people, given to maintaining the truth of the Bible. Satan through his people would seek to destroy the message of the church. Only a separated people can be true guardians of the sacred doctrines.

This was graphically demonstrated to me by a mulch pile. I had a desire to use less commercial fertilizer by replacing it with good mulch. I established a mulch pile, putting into it kitchen vegetable scraps and the unused parts from the vegetables in my garden. In the spring I spread the resulting mulch on the garden.

I was surprised how little mulch I had made. Knowing I had to increase the material going into the pile, I considered lawn clippings. However, the previous year I had used a commercial lawn service to help develop a lush, weed-free lawn. I decided it would be safer to wait a year before I used the grass clippings, in order to ensure the chemicals were completely leached out of the lawn. As a result I turned to a second source. I would use the weeds I pulled from my garden beds.

The second year, I spread the mulch on the garden. In a few weeks, I saw the error of my ways. I had planted weed seeds abundantly. They had not rotted properly in the mulch pile. I had to spend many hours on my knees correcting the situation. As a result of the experience, I carefully separated the weeds from the good material. Never again would I introduce evil into my garden.

In the second verse, there is a promise we should take to heart. God promises to be our Father and assures us we will be His children. Notice it is a conditional promise. It is after we come out and are a separated people we become His children. God desires a serious commitment on our part in order to enjoy the privilege of being family.

Let us learn a lesson from the mulch pile. We need to be very careful not to introduce evil into the garden of faith. Let's not imitate Lot's wife and retain desires to go back to our roots.

Father, again we thank you for the simplicity of the lessons found in our gardens. We truly appreciate Your teaching us profound truths in easy to understand ways. Strengthen our resolve to be a separated people. We ask it in the name of Christ. Amen.

DAY 17
DEAD PLANTS BRING FORTH ABUNDANTLY

Knowing this, that our old man is crucified with him, that the body of sin might be destroyed, that henceforth we should not serve sin. (Romans 6:6)

Thought for the day:
Plants allowed to decay and become mulch provide the food for new growth. The new creature in Christ must be fed properly. The best food is the decayed, old nature.

Yesterday, I shared with you the disaster brought to my garden due to the weeds I had introduced into the mulch pile. Their seeds had not rotted into mulch. When I put the mulch on the garden, I ended up planting weed seeds among my vegetables. I paid a heavy price in increased weeding as a result of my negligence.

As I learned from my mistakes, I began to produce good mulch. I carefully checked everything going into the pile. To increase the amount of mulch, I added the clippings from the lawn and the leaves from trees. Keeping it well watered, and turning it often, resulted in a rich black mulch. Every spring, this mulch would be spread on the garden prior to tilling. Its effect was excellent. My plants grew and produced abundantly. I was able to eliminate all commercial fertilizer, saving money, while ensuring an adequate food supply for the length of the growing season. All the dead, decayed plants produced healthy, beautiful new plants with an excellent yield.

Meditating upon God's Word, I realized the mulch pile illustrated two valuable, positive lessons. These lessons are vital to our personal Christian growth, and the fruitfulness of our lives. If we are to obtain onto the standard Christ has delineated, we must become human mulch piles.

Becoming a mulch pile centers around our ability to die to self, allowing our fleshy nature and lusts to decay. Only when we lay aside all of our personal desires will we be able to become a new creation. Just as the plants in the mulch pile had to decay and take on a new nature, we too must follow their example. Self must be taken to the cross and crucified.

Jesus tells us it is a daily process. Every day there is the tendency of self to rise up and take control. No matter how long we have been a Christian, or how spiritual we try to act, our human nature wants to exert itself.

It was this nature which originally led to the fall of Adam and Eve. They wanted to be in control, know what the gods knew, make their own decisions. Nobody should have to tell them what was right or wrong. That nature is still trying to assert itself today. Man is no different today. Human nature hasn't changed.

Christian growth consists of learning to crucify our self-sufficient attitudes, placing ourselves totally under the direction of the Trinity. It is not easy to fight oneself. Yet, in essence, that is exactly what we are called upon to do. We have to take self-determination, self-desires, and self-sufficiency to the cross. Nailed there daily, it will die a slow, excruciating death.

Eventually, albeit agonizingly slow, self will begin to decay and Christ will come shining through. The old man has rotted and become a mulch pile. In its place there comes forth new growth fertilized by that which has died. Sin no longer reins over our lives.

We are totally surrendered to the will of God. Life has new meaning and objectives. The plant of the new creation grows strong and beautiful.

As I searched my memory for a good example of a man who had crucified his old nature, I settled on the Apostle John. Here was a rough fisherman. He had a nickname, "Son of Thunder", which reflected his nature. John wanted to call down fire from heaven and destroy a city. There was no room for forgiveness. Act quick and show them what's what was part of his makeup. He also was a man who wanted to be a leader and sit on the right hand of Christ, when He set up His Kingdom. No third place relationship would satisfy John. He wanted to be on top.

That was the old John, before he had crucified self. Later, as we read his Gospel and epistles, we find a completely different human being. He became the Apostle of love. Tolerance, forgiveness, proper respect for others, concern for their welfare are all evident in this new creature. The nature of Christ came to full bloom, as the old John decayed and became a mulch pile.

Each and every Christian needs to experience the same transformation. Only as we throw self on the mulch pile, can we begin to exhibit the fruits of the Spirit. As long as the old man remains, our nature will be like the old John. A new nature cannot experience proper growth, until the old becomes mulch.

The second lesson I learned from the mulch pile concerns the productivity achieved from proper mulching. The mulch provided a steady supply of food for the whole season. It didn't leach out of the ground like commercial fertilizer. My plants grew, looked better, and produced more abundantly as a result of having a proper food supply.

Our fruitfulness as a Christian will increase dramatically as self decays and Christ grows. In fact, Jesus tells us we cannot produce any fruit, unless He abides within us. Anything we attempt will be to no avail. Christ must be in total control. Deeds undertaken while under the control of self, will only tend to glorify self. Deeds taken under the control of Christ will glorify Him. As a result, they will be abundantly fruitful. He can be in total control only when the old self has become a mulch pile.

In order to make good mulch, there are two important requirements. It must be kept well watered, and it must be constantly turned. This allows all of the material to thoroughly decay. I learned this as a result of another one of my mistakes. One year, I didn't pay much attention to the mulch pile. I just dumped stuff on it. In the spring, much of the material hadn't rotted. The amount of mulch available was substantially reduced. From then on, I made it a point to maintain a regular schedule of watering and turning the mulch pile.

The old man requires the same treatment if it is to properly transform itself into valuable material. The watering comes from daily Bible reading, praying, fellowshipping with other Christians. They provide the environment for the decaying process. The stirring comes from God. He is always working, making sure the mulch pile thoroughly decays. Self must be destroyed. Only God has the insight into our nature which can bring it to pass.

The faith heroes in the Bible are prime examples of what it means to die to self. As we read about them, their dependency upon God is ever present. They are always conversing with Him, asking for His direction, and obeying His every command.

However, on occasion, we see their old nature trying to exert itself. When it does, God intervenes in some way. Jonah had to go into a fish's belly. Job had to suffer the loss of wealth and family. David had to be hunted by Saul. Abraham had to leave family and friends. Moses tended sheep. Paul had to be blinded. Peter had to be humbled by a rooster. The decaying process continued, bringing them back to their proper relationship with Him.

The decayed old man is the mulch for a new life in Christ. It allows Him to grow in our lives, producing abundant fruit. May we all work at getting the old man to the mulch pile and decayed properly. It is the only way to proper growth. As long as self remains in control, Christ will be a weak, anemic plant. A decayed self, produces strong growth.

Father, we do want to manifest the life of Christ. We are shamefully aware of how much of self remains. Please continue to stir the mulch pile, destroying every vestige of old vegetation, that Christ might grow in the new man. Speed the rotting process, so we can experience the thrill of having Christ in total control. We desire to be fruitful plants. Father, thank you for the truth of the mulch pile. I praise you in Jesus' name. Amen.

DAY 18
GARDENS REVEAL THE EXISTENCE OF GOD

Because that which may be known of God is manifest in them; for God hath shewed it unto them. For the invisible things of him from the creation of the world are clearly seen, being understood by the things that are made, even his eternal power and Godhead; so that they are without excuse: (Romans 1:19-20)

Thought for the day:
God has expressed Himself in all of creation. Observing the garden we understand a little of what God is like. It humbles us to know He included us in His plan.

The Creator God has gone to great lengths to make sure every person on the face of the earth knows He exists. Even if someone never hears about God, they will have no excuse for not seeking Him out. His creation will stand as a testimony against them.

Any defense will be rejected by the Heavenly Judge. He will say to them, "Why didn't you learn from the earth, plants, and animals that I existed? They all testify of me. They reveal my power, wisdom, eternal nature. All you had to do was meditate upon them. It would have brought you to the conclusion that I exist and created all things. I find you guilty!"

We do not have to view the whole creation to see the proof of God's existence. My gardens often speak to me concerning the reality of an eternal, wise, loving Father. While working in the garden, I often meditate on how well it reflects God. From weeds, to beautiful flowers, to nourishing vegetables, God is revealing something about His nature.

I often feel sorry for those who believe in evolution. They blind themselves to some of the richest truths. Even worse, is the way they insist on teaching others the fallacy of their ways. We often use the term, "the blind leading the blind". In the case of these instructors, they go beyond mere leading. They are creating new blind creatures. Indoctrinating them with their heresy, they are forever closing young minds to the possibility of a God who cares. Unfortunately, these young people end up paying a terrible price in this life, plus an eternal price of endless suffering.

When I look at the beauty of the flowers, I see a God of beauty. God could have created us with a monochrome vision like so many of the animals. All we would have been able to see would have been black and white shapes. He could have created all plants with the same color bloom, or no bloom at all. In either case the world would have appeared to us as a very drab place to live. Instead, God wanted man to appreciate Him and the beauty He represents. What better way, than to give him lovely flowers. Their varied shapes and colors reflect a God of great beauty.

As a boy, I loved to wander the fields and pastures. They contained beauty beyond description. I would pick bouquets of flowers for Mom. The wild flowers consisted of varied colored paint brush, daisies, black-eyed susans, buttercups, and anything else that would be in bloom. God's garden always had something of beauty to offer.

I think it was from those early attempts to give my Mother something beautiful, that I learned to appreciate inter-mingling of color. Later, I carried that characteristic into my flower beds. I love beds with a lot of color all inter-twined. As I take time to appreciate their beauty, I try to imagine what the beauty of Heaven will be like. I confess, it is beyond my imagination. I just know that a God of beauty will have the most beautiful place waiting when we arrive there.

Looking over my vegetable garden, I see a God who cares. God could have given us a very limited appetite. We would have eaten grass, or a certain kind of fruit or vegetable. Most animals have a very limited diet, yet they grow and are healthy. Man could have been created in the same way. But a God who cares, wanted Man to be able to break out of the mundane. Wide and varied foods add excitement to our everyday existence.

Man was instilled with God's creativity, having been made in His image. Therefore, man should be allowed to express himself. By utilizing various vegetables in our cuisine, God has allowed us to feel the joy of creativity. As we create new dishes, we can begin to experience the joy God must have received as He created. It helps us to understand all of this could not just have happened. It had to be planned by a God who cares.

When I meditate upon the varied ways the fruits and vegetables grow, I see a God with infinite abilities. Nothing is too impossible for a God who is able to create numerous shapes and methods of growth. Clumps of bananas, ears of corn, and pods of peas speak of God's ability to package the product in different ways. Growing on trees, vines, bushes, or in the ground demonstrates His ability to produce good things in any way He deems necessary. Sweet or tart, hard or soft, rich in a particular vitamin or mineral illustrates His ability to create products for different needs. What tremendous capabilities,

God has. How can we not appreciate Him?

Looking at the various plants in by gardens, I see a God of infinite wisdom. Each plant is shaped in a very specific way. They bloom at a time table exactly fitted to their need to reproduce. They have different shaped leaves, flowers, stems, and root systems. Their environment is diverse: growing in wet or dry soil, on rocks, trees, and in the dirt. Each plant is perfectly designed to grow and reproduce. They each have a place in the whole scheme of God's creation. They reflect the wisdom of God.

As I view the various insects gathered in the garden, I appreciate the carefulness with which God planned it all. Various insects feed on various plants, ignoring others which are food for other species. Some insects actually benefit the plant by pollinating it, or providing a defense against a particular type of insect infestation. All is kept in a delicate balance. Truly, this could only have occurred as a result of a "master plan".

Scientists now tell us, plants have built in systems which allow them to protect themselves against insect and disease infestations. Some develop chemicals which cause the insect to become ill. Others have the ability to communicate among themselves. Trees under attack will warn other trees of the same specie in the immediate vicinity, allowing them to prepare for the attack before it arrives. Only a God, capable of planning it to the most infinite detail could have developed our world and provided for its continued existence.

Evolutionists certainly miss the point when they say this all happened. Things that happen end up a mess. Things that are planned, fit together in infinite detail and ways. All of nature is calling us to look at the symmetry and inter-relationships of plants to the rest of nature and see there the requirement for a master planner to put it all together.

Every time I visit my gardens, I appreciate God more. He has gone to great lengths to demonstrate His power, wisdom, and presence. From the beauty of the rose, the fragrance of the lilac, the magnificent shapes of the lilies, God is trying to tell us He exists. Venturing into the fields to appreciate the wild flowers, God speaks about how carefully He designed it all. They are capable of growing and reproducing without any helping hand from a gardener. The Master Gardener has provided for them. He also has provided for us. I then realize, His plan included me.

My gardens and the flowers of the field humble me. Seeing the depth of planning God put into all of His creation, I wonder why He called me to be His achild. I know I am not worthy of such a honor. God could have created something more worthy to receive His image and to be indwelt by His Spirit. But, he didn't. He called me. I can only kneel before Him in appreciation.

Father, I thank you for the plants of the fields and my gardens. They do speak of your magnificence. Knowing you gave us this creation as a testimony to yourself, I am humbled before you. Lord, I pray for those who fail to see You in creation. Soften their hearts and open their eyes. They need to be able to appreciate your glory. I praise you in Jesus' name. Amen.

DAY 19
SOME PLANTS FAIL TO PRODUCE

And now also the axe is laid unto the root of the trees: every tree therefore which bringeth not forth good fruit is hewn down, and cast into the fire. (Luke 3:9)

Thought for the day:
We plant fruit trees expecting to reap a harvest. The Lord plants souls hoping to reap a similar harvest. Only His patience keeps Him from hewing down unfruitful trees.

When I reached the age of fourteen, Dad took me squirrel hunting. I became hooked. Every weekend would find us out in the woods hunting some type of game. We would leave at seven in the morning and return at five in the evening. Our lunches were carried with us. We did not want to miss a single minute of hunting. From the start of hunting season in October, to its conclusion at the end of February, we could only be found in some woodland.

The forests in our area had an abundance of apple trees. Some had grown wild, while others gave evidence of being some early settlers' apple orchard. Since squirrels, deer, and partridge fed under these trees, we became very familiar with their location. We not only hunted these areas, we usually picked an apple to chew. Most were very bitter, but we were able to find trees producing fruit with a delightful flavor. There was nothing quite so good as one of those apples picked fresh from the tree. It became standard routine for us to head for these trees to supplement the sandwiches we carried in our pouches.

    Later in my adult years, after I had moved from the area, the craving for fresh apples right off of the tree enticed me to buy some dwarf fruit trees. I planted two apples and a cherry. The catalog indicated it would be three years before I would start to see them produce. The trees were fed, watered, and dusted with great care. They prospered under the tender, loving care given them. Two growing seasons seemed to drag by. It was with great expectation I looked forward to the next growing season.

    During the fall following the second summer, a minor disaster struck in the form of a bad rain and wind storm. One of my apple trees partially blew over. I went out to inspect it and quickly saw the reason for its inability to bear up under the wind. One of its main roots had been attacked by some insect and eaten through. Still, the plant had two other good roots. I determined I would make an attempt to save the tree, hoping it might develop another root to replace the one destroyed. I reset it, and braced it against the coming winter season. However, I knew the tree was set back for several years before it would start to produce.

    The next spring, my remaining two trees gave great promise of bearing. They blossomed profusely. A few weeks later I realized my cherry tree had failed to set any fruit. Nevertheless, the remaining apple tree had seven apples starting to form. I maintained a close eye on their development. Two fell prematurely for some reason. The other five grew and were nearing maturity.

    On one of my inspection trips, I saw disaster had hit again. A deer had taken one bite out of each apple. All five were lost. I was ready to take the axe to all three trees. The effort put forth was not worth the return. Even if they did eventually start to produce, I had no assurance they would escape the deer. The trees had become completely worthless. The axe should be put to their roots. They at least would make good firewood. Then, I could divert my efforts toward more promising garden projects.

The Lord must feel that way with us sometimes. He nourishes, cares, and watches over us with the greatest concern and anticipation. He wants to see the fruit of His efforts, and it is never forth coming. He must get very disappointed and frustrated in our lack of fruitfulness.

There are three types of fruit the Lord wants in our life. They are personal maturity, souls won to the Lord, and edification of other Christians. When these are achieved in our lives, they become real contentment and a special offering unto our Savior. We have returned to Him, a reward for the efforts He has made on our behalf.

Personal maturity is the beginning point for a fruitful Christian. The other two fruits cannot appear until the Christian has come to maturity. My dwarf trees had to grow for three years, before I could expect them to produce. Likewise, the Christian must grow before he can produce. Only healthy, full-grown trees can be expected to bear.

Personal growth involves more than just a growth in knowledge. We can become totally familiar with the Bible, able to quote numerous verses. However, knowledge is only the fertilizer for the true growth. It is only when we start to reflect that knowledge in our attitudes, prayer life, and relationships with others, we near the point where we can bear the other kinds of fruit.

Most of us have met people with a fairly good understanding of what is contained in the Bible. However, their lives are like the blown down apple tree. Their roots are decayed. The joy of their salvation is missing from their souls. They have an abrasiveness which makes you want to stay clear of them. Minor problems become major battlefields. They are easily hurt by the smallest of offenses. No matter how much time is spent in trying to get them to develop new roots, they just never attain unto maturity. They are worth more as firewood. At least the churches' efforts could be directed toward more promising areas.

We also have met individuals who have developed new attitudes. They are pleasant to be around. There is a joy in their hearts and a smile on their faces. However, they are like my cherry tree. They are beautiful trees come to maturity, yet they never set any fruit. They do not participate in edifying the body of believers or winning souls to the Lord. For various reasons, they are not able to function in a productive way. The Lord's effort, while not entirely wasted, is never fully rewarded. My cherry tree was beautiful in bloom, but productive. So are they.

There is a third type of unproductive Christian. They are similar to the apple tree which set fruit for the deer. These Christians mature and begin to win souls and edify the church. However, their efforts are eaten up through over work. They spread themselves too thin. Eventually, their fruit is destroyed by outside influences and never comes to being fully satisfying to the Lord. They become disenchanted and give up. Their usefulness falls to the level of becoming firewood.

I am not sure my dwarf trees ever did produce. We sold our house, and a year later moved to a new state. Just prior to moving, we drove by the house and noticed the new owners had cut down several trees I had nurtured in my front lawn. The fruit trees were in back of the house and couldn't be seen. I suspect they too became the victim of the axe. Given their record of fruit producing, I would not fault the buyer, if he had made them into firewood. At least, he would have gotten some benefit from them.

I am just glad our Lord is patient with us. If He wasn't, I am afraid many of us would end up as firewood. But, our God is a much better, more industrious gardener than we are. He will continue to fertilize, tend, and watch over His orchard. Even one tree brought to full fruit bearing will give Him great pleasure. Over time, His garden will produce fruit. The axe will be slow to strike.

Father, May we each examine our lives and determine what type of fruit tree we are becoming. May our lives develop solid roots as our attitudes change. Lead us to the point of becoming productive soul winners and body builders. Keep us from becoming tired and discouraged. May we use Your example of patience and untiring efforts as the plumb line for productivity. Thank you for the failed dwarf fruit trees. They communicated a vital message. We love and adore you. We ask it in Jesus' name. Amen.

DAY 20
NEGLECT JUST HAPPENS

Wherefore I put thee in remembrance that thou stir up the gift of God, which is in thee by the putting on of my hands. (II Timothy 1:6)

Thought for the day:
Plants die as a result of neglect. Christian growth dies in the same manner. In the end, our garden and God's garden loses some of its beauty.

I was introduced to irises at an early age. They were one of my mother's favorite flowers gracing a long bed across the front of the house. On one occasion, she took me to a neighboring town where a man grew extensive gardens of iris. This individual showed us how he would take pollen from one particular iris and use it to fertilize another as he attempted to produce new colors. I was fascinated with his work. I immediately developed a short lived conviction, it might be something I would like to do.

I never did follow up on propagating iris. In fact, I never really learned much about how to grow them. Other than rare attempts at trying to keep the weeds pulled, Mom's flower gardens suffered from neglect. Through the summer months on a farm, there was too much work. She had to help in the fields, grow and preserve fruits and vegetables, while attempting to keep her daily housework under control. Even with all the neglect, the iris managed to bloom every year. Their beauty made a lasting impression.

In developing one of my flower beds, I decided it was about time to plant some iris. I had a perfect spot from which to show them off. Their blooms would give the garden real pizzazz. Out came the seed catalog order form. I ordered several rhizomes capable of producing giant blooms. On their arrival, they were quickly planted and hovered over like a mother hen.

I was not disappointed. During the next two years, the iris gave forth some of the most gigantic, gorgeous blooms I had ever seen. They had made my efforts worthwhile. However, near disaster was about to strike.

I had no knowledge on growing and maintaining iris. My mother's always seemed to survive in spite of the neglect, so other than weeding and spring fertilizing, I did nothing. One day, while working in the flower beds, I noticed one group of iris rhizomes was rotting. I was panic stricken and started to check the others. I found two more showing signs of decay.

Almost instantly, I recalled seeing people who had cut back and separated their iris after they were done blooming. I suspected, the decay was being caused by the overcrowding of the rhizomes. The rest of the morning was spent in digging up each grouping, cutting out the decaying parts, separating them into smaller groups, and replanting in various beds. Fortunately, I had discovered the problem in time. The next season, I was doubly blessed with their beauty and increased number of groupings.

As I was dividing the rhizomes, I started thinking about what caused their near demise. I recognized lack of knowledge was part of the problem. Yet, I had garden books I could have checked. In just minutes I could have become well informed on growing these plants. I was a busy man, but I still had time to weed the gardens and do the other necessary work. I could have found time to divide them. The real problem was just plain neglect. I hadn't made a commitment to really make sure my iris prospered. They had been planted and left to grow on their own. My mother's neglected beds had become my neglected beds.

How well those iris reflect our Christian lives. Neglect often takes a heavy toll. Neglect is seldom planned. Neither do we take the time to make sure it is planned against. Neglect happens because we let it happen. Instead of taking charge of the situation, we become lackadaisical. All of a sudden, our spiritual lives start to rot.

Each of us has the responsibility to plan our paths away from the road of neglect. On some regular basis, we should take a few minutes and plan our spiritual growth. A brief analysis of our spiritual needs will reveal where we need to spend more time. We then can set aside specific time slots for meeting those needs.

We might recognize a lack of Bible knowledge. The solution might be a regular time each day for Bible study. If we find ourselves incapable of learning by ourselves, we could seek out one or more weekly Bible studies. Recognizing the need is the hard part. Once the need is seen, the solution normally is found very easily.

Instead of needing Bible knowledge, we might see a need for more prayer time, fellowshipping with other Christians, or singing of praises. Regardless of the need, a plan of action should then be mapped out. But a plan by itself is insufficient.

The plan must be put into action and regularly followed.

It is the action part where we are most apt to see neglect set in. There are so many things which can easily creep into our lives. Work, entertainment, family problems, outside activities all combine to squeeze out the action part of our spiritual growth plan. Until we recognize our spiritual growth is more important than all of the others put together, we will subject our spiritual lives to unnecessary neglect.

The crux of a spiritual growth plan is to establish it as the top priority of our lives. However, most of us fail to see its importance in that light. We so easily allow everything else to take charge. Life in the natural realm always seems to be more important. Our natural life is a few short years, while our spiritual life is for eternity. Therefore, it should receive first place in all considerations.

A second major problem of neglect is its tendency to be transferable. Mom's neglect of her iris convinced me they could be neglected and nothing would happen. The way we tend our spiritual lives will influence others. We need to be concerned about the positive or negative effect we have on other Christians.

Neglect transference is especially a danger for Christians in leadership positions. If a congregation sees their Pastor, Deacons, Elders, and Sunday School teachers neglecting their spiritual lives, they will readily come to the conclusion there is no need for a spiritual plan. Way too often, bowling, hunting, swimming, television, sports all take priority over spiritual growth. How devastating this is to the young Christian. They have no perfect role model to follow. In the end, their spiritual roots will decay as my iris rhizomes decayed.

Even the Bibles' saints had problems with neglect. Apparently Paul was afraid Timothy had a problem in this area. In the second letter to his close friend, he encouraged Timothy to stir up the gift he received by the laying on of hands. He wanted Timothy to make sure the Holy Spirit was totally in charge of his life. Neglect of this vital source of power would severely limit Timothy's work. Paul was calling Him to get his priorities in order and develop a spiritual growth plan to destroy the monster of neglect. May Paul's urging speak to our hearts as well.

Why not take a few extra minutes right now and develop a spiritual growth plan. Your life will bloom more abundantly, and your influence on others will become a positive force in their lives. I was doubly blessed by my iris when I took proper action. We each can be blessed ten-fold over when we take proper spiritual action by planning, executing and giving priority to our spiritual growth plan. We can become beautiful blooms in God's garden, multiplying our growth through many flower beds.

Father: Don't let our spiritual lives go into decay. Stir us up. Give us a desire to create and execute a spiritual growth plan. Make sure we understand its importance. Rather than decaying, we want to become blooms in your garden. Please help us. We pray it in the name of Jesus. Amen.

DAY 21
GOD'S GIFT TO PLANTS

> *And God said, Let the earth bring forth grass, the herb yielding seed, and the fruit tree yielding fruit after his kind, whose seed is in itself, upon the earth; and it was so. And the earth brought forth grass, and herb yielding seed after his kind, and the tree yielding fruit, whose seed was in itself, after his kind: and God saw that it was good.* (Genesis 1:11-12)

Thought for the day:
Through the diversity of plant reproduction we have further evidence of creation. It is another way God has attempted to reveal Himself to mankind.

Recently, while doing some weeding, I started to think about the various ways plants propagate themselves. Some do it through an extensive root system sending up new shoots along its length. Others, guarantee the survival of the species by multiplying their bulbs and rhizomes. Still others reproduce by cross pollinating and producing seeds. Sometimes the wind provides the means for pollination, while insects or birds provide it for other plants. Some plants use their own pollen, while others need a plant of the opposite sex. Seeds are scattered in diverse ways. They blow, stick, or are carried to other sites. Each plant has its own means of reproduction. Each method produces the desired result.

I found the subject fascinating and started to meditate upon its significance in God's creation. To me, it became one more proof of God's existence and another nail in the coffin of evolution. The diversity of their reproductive systems and their dependency upon the elements and other creatures for their survival create astronomical numerical odds against the slightest possibility of evolution.

The evolutionist would have us accept certain concepts as being the very basis for their beliefs. They are: (1) the survival of the fittest, (2) change occurred slowly over long periods of time as each living organism found a better way to survive, and (3) all living organisms evolved from a few simple life forms. Let us examine these concepts against the record of creation as found in the ways plants propagate their kind.

If only one or two living plant organisms appeared upon the face of the earth and started to evolve into other plants, we are faced with several problems.

First: If only the fittest survived, all unfit plants would have had to die out. Therefore, only a few plants as they evolved could have made it down through the millions of years the evolutionist would have us believe was necessary. Those failing to evolve along the same lines as the survivors would have been unfit for their environment. Many plants live and reproduce under very limited environmental conditions. Their existence would have terminated quickly as the environment changed and prevented them from reproducing. They would not have had time to slowly evolve to a point where they were capable of living under less than ideal conditions. However, we have tens of thousands of plants, each capable of surviving in a different environment.

Second: Somewhere during the line of evolution, various species of plants would have had to decide how they were going to reproduce. Can you imagine two holly plants getting together and carrying on a conversation along the following lines.

"I'm tired of sending out long root systems in order to grow new plants. Why don't we try to develop a new way of reproducing?"

"Fine, I'm game. Do you have anything particular in mind?"

"Well, I thought we might develop something called sex. It would require a male and a female to mate in some way in order to produce seeds capable of reproducing our specie."

"Oh. What do male and female look like, and how are they to mate? Also, what do seeds look like and how are they structured?"

"I haven't fully developed the concept yet. But why don't you start to become a male holly, and I'll become a female. In a hundred thousand years or so, we'll get together and see if we can produce a seed. Okay?"

"Why not? Good luck. See you in a hundred thousand years!"

It can become quite amusing as one contemplates how two plants of the same specie could develop along entirely different lines, yet in a manner that would make them totally compatible to each other in order to reproduce seeds capable of carrying their combined traits and sex into future generations.

It would be impossible for two plants to evolve sexual organs capable of inter-relating to each other. But then to have them develop the ability to transfer their characteristics to a new thing called a seed stretches the odds to infinity. Add to this, the necessity of both male and female plants having to evolve at the same point in time, and the odds go beyond infinity.

Third: The distribution of seeds through the utilization of animals and the elements creates another problem for the evolutionist. Some plants are totally dependent upon a given specie for the distribution of their seeds. Had the distributor not evolved, the plant would never have been able to propagate.

In many cases, the plant and the distributor of the seeds are inter-dependent upon each other. The plant needs the specie to distribute its seeds, while the distributor needs the plant for food. Therefore, both species would have had to evolve at the same time. Furthermore, as they evolved, they would have had to evolve along lines which would make each of them cognizant of the other. Obviously, this becomes a total impossibility without some master mind developing the inter-relationship and awareness.

As an example, consider an insect which graces all of our gardens, the common bee. In order for the plant to transfer its pollen into the proper receptacle, the bee becomes vitally important. Without the transfer, no seeds would be produced, and the plant would vanish from the earth. However, the bee needs plants to produce the nectar they utilize in honey production for food and propagation of their species.

Imagine a plant saying to itself, "Well, I'll produce some nectar, which will attract some bees so they can transfer my pollen and cause me to make seeds in order to reproduce my kind." Sounds kind of ridiculous, doesn't it. Now add to that the bee's comments, "I'll go get some nectar that plant is going to produce and transform it into honey in order to provide food for myself and developing young." Complicate this by the hundreds of inter-dependent relationships and it becomes readily apparent of the impossibility of this just happening. It had to be carefully planned.

To all of this, add the various ways plants have developed their seeds for distribution. Can you imagine a plant deciding to make a seed pod capable of sticking to the fur of an animal so it could be carried to another point? Other plants would have decided to produce seeds as food, but in such an abundance the animals feeding on them would waste enough or hide enough to ensure the reproduction of the plant. Then the plants utilizing the wind for distribution had to plan elaborate seed systems capable of being borne by the wind. It gets more and more complicated and harder to imagine it could have just happened.

Studying plants, especially their diversity and inter-dependency of reproduction deepens my faith in the creativity of our God. He has gone to great lengths to ensure mankind realizes He was responsible for all of creation. It took intelligence and great planning to put together a world as complex as the one in which we dwell. God's creative acts flash at us from every nook and cranny of our gardens. It is another example of the extreme to which God has gone to reveal Himself to mankind

Father, we thank You for the evidence of Your creative acts as found in our gardens. We praise You for Your efforts to reveal Yourself to our blind eyes. Truly, You are a God that wants man to know You. Thank You in the name of Jesus. Amen.

DAY 22
STRAIGHT LINES ARE MUCH NICER

Brethren, be followers together of me, and mark them which walk so as ye have us for an ensample. (For many walk, of whom I have told you often, and now tell you even weeping, that they are the enemies of the cross of Christ:
(Philippians 3:17-18)

And make straight paths for your feet,
(Hebrews 12:13a)

Thought for the day:
To make straight lines, we have to use some type of guide line. In our spiritual life, the guide line is the Lord Jesus. We make our paths according to His life.

The spring had been a wet and cold one, delaying the planting of my vegetable garden. Finally, the weather broke and I hurriedly prepared the seed bed. Once it was ready, due to the press of time, I decided I wouldn't take the time to put a guideline across the garden for making rows. It would save a few minutes. If I was careful using the previous row as a guideline, I should accomplish the task rather easily. As dusk settled over the earth, the last seeds were covered. I sat back to let nature takes its course.

With all the rain we had, the seeds sprouted and grew quickly. One morning, looking out of our second story bedroom, I was struck by a sudden attack of seasickness. The green vegetables showed the crookedness of my rows. They looked like waves on the sea. I vowed never again to take a shortcut in making rows.

Everything we do in life requiring a straight line, necessitates using some type of guideline. The same need applies to our spiritual life. To satisfy the need, Father has seen fit to provide us with several guidelines. They are, in order of importance, Christ, the Bible, and the lives of mature saints. Using them, will keeps our rows from getting out of alignment.

Christ is the perfect guideline. He has set examples for us in every area of life. If we would constantly measure our life against his standard, we could avoid a lot of trouble for ourselves, the church, and the body of Christ. To see the necessity of straight spiritual paths, view the news media. They are carrying numerous stories of improper Christian conduct. It opens the church up to all sorts of criticism.

Now as never before in the history of our country, the Christian church is under attack from many directions. Government, the ACLU, religious sects, news media, false prophets, individuals, all directed by Satan are doing their best to bring the church into disrepute. However, their success will be minor compared to the disaster Christians will bring upon themselves. We do more to shame the name of Christ than any other organization.

The name of Christ is being subjected to ridicule on almost a daily basis. This shouldn't be! The church should be the most straight organization on the face of the earth. It has the most perfect straight line in the person of Christ. We just aren't using the straightedge to set the guidelines. Like my garden rows, we take a chance hoping things will come out right. In the process we create a lot of waves for the media to ride.

Let us consider the examples Christ has set before us. They will stand us in good stead today and every day. More importantly, they will bring a renewal to the church, and possible revival to the land.

First: Consider how He lived His life. He never sinned. His life was totally pure. If only we would make an attempt to be as clean. We are more apt to look at the sins of others, rather than at our own blackness. Pointing fingers will never clean up our lives. It only putrefies them more. Nightly introspection of all we did and said during the day will soon teach us the necessity of stopping and thinking before we act.

Most of us are too lazy to try for a pure life. Purity requires work, sin comes very easily. Being spiritual couch-potatoes, we enjoy the ease of sin. If we are going to work at purity, we have to spend time reading the Bible, analyzing our lives, and weeping before the throne. Recreation, and idle time will need to be bypassed in favor of purity building activities. It won't be pleasant, it will be rewarding.

Second: Consider how he treated sinners. His life reflects He treated sinners in two different ways. To the repentant sinner, He was forgiving and gracious. To the unrepentant, He was harsh in His condemnation of their activities.

The church needs to take a much firmer stand against sinful activities. The barriers are in bad need of strengthening. The modern church has lowered its standards considerably. Activities which would have come under condemnation thirty years ago, now are permitted and even recognized as being legitimate. Christ would never have done this. Only the repentant person would have gained His favor. He expected them to reach up to His standard, not He lower Himself to theirs.

Third: Consider his courage. He never backed down from stating His case clearly and forthrightly. He never was afraid of what the world could do to Him. When it came time for Him to pay the price for our sin, He resolutely set His face toward Jerusalem. Standing before the tribunal about to sentence Him to death, He offered no defense. Hanging on the cross, He refused to call down a legion of angels to set Him free.

If only our churches, leaders, and individual members would exhibit the same degree of courage. Somewhere along the way, living in peace and security, has replaced Christ's example of taking on the world. We fear to take stands. We stay within our white buildings, seated on our comfortable pews, enjoying the pulpit entertainment, rather than becoming a driving force for change. Our life of ease has given the anti-Christian forces free reign. Their influence on government has climbed steadily, while our influence has waned. Slowly, the church's importance is being pushed into the background.

Paul, in writing to the Philippi church, had concerns along these same lines. He called his readers to become fellow-imitators of the Lord Jesus. Just as he and others had patterned their lives after Christ, he wanted the whole church to copy their pattern. In doing so, the life of Christ would be manifested throughout the area. Great glory would be won for the name of Christ.

Paul reminded his readers, there were many who walked in ways other than the standard of Christ. He wrote that it caused him to weep. This was followed by a startling statement. He called them the enemies of the cross of Christ.

Can you imagine Christians becoming the enemies of the cross? In essence, it is exactly what happens when we fail to live to the standard of Christ's example. When we allow purity and righteousness to decay in our lives, Satan wins. We have helped his kingdom, instead of the kingdom of Christ. Every time we allow Satan to win a battle, the cross and Christ's sacrifice become less meaningful. We have become its enemy, not its ally.

Christ desires, and Paul recognized, the need for every church to have living examples in their body. Christians new to the faith need those examples. We each have the capability of becoming that example. We not only have the capability, we have the responsibility. Christ is an example, not to view, but to imitate.

Let us keep our rows straight. Don't imitate me in making crooked garden rows. I was in a hurry, and didn't think I could go too far astray. I proved myself wrong. Our spiritual rows can only be kept straight by following Christ in every activity. Let us not deceive ourselves by hurrying through life without Christ. We can go wrong and make crooked paths. We don't need more seasick Christians. Straight paths will prevent the problem.

Father: May we never become enemies of the cross. Instead, help us to make our paths straight. Keep our hearts teachable, our conscience tender, and our minds determined. We would become living examples of Christ. We ask if for His glory. Amen.

DAY 23
FIELD CORN ISN'T SWEET CORN

If there come any unto you, and bring not this doctrine, receive him not into your house, neither bid him God speed: For he that biddeth him God speed is partaker of his evil deeds. (II John 10-11)

Beware lest any man spoil you through philosophy and vain deceit, after the tradition of men, after the rudiments of the world, and not after Christ.
(Colossians 2:8)

Thought for the day:
We can package a product attractively, but the product may be lacking in quality. Christ is concerned about how we package His gospel. He wants sweetness on the inside, not high-tech designed packages.

My grandfather owned a dairy farm. To feed the cows through the winter, hay and corn silage was harvested and stored. The farmers in the neighborhood were always ready to help one another. It was quite common for them to go from farm to farm as crops matured and assist in the reaping. Usually there was no money exchanged. A day's work given would be a day's work received in return. However, they normally were given a hearty dinner.

I remember one occasion when I was helping with the reaping of oats. There were about eight neighbors helping out. My grandmother and mother prepared a big meal. We had pot-roast, mashed potatoes, gravy, corn-on-the-cob, and two kinds of pie. The serving bowls were heaped high, for these mighty eaters.

For some reason, my grandfather had failed to plant sweet corn that year. Instead, they used the ears of the field corn they were growing for silage. The long, golden ears were coming into their "milk". They were delicious looking. There, of course, was an apology from grandmother for having to serve field corn and not sweet corn. The neighbors were all gracious in return. They commented on how juicy and tender it was, and expressed their appreciation for such a fine meal.

However, when I bit into one of the ears, I knew it wasn't sweet corn. The kernels were big and they were tough, regardless of what the neighbors said. The taste was blah. The sweetness one was accustomed to was missing. The field corn wasn't sweet corn, no matter how much you pretended that it was.

When I started to develop ideas for this book, the Holy Spirit called to mind this incident of long ago. At first, I couldn't understand why. It didn't seem to have much connection with learning from God's kingdom. The more I thought about it, the more I realized there were two tremendous truths being revealed: (1) the packaging doesn't make the product; (2) what's on the inside is what really counts.

There is a trend in the modern church which concerns me greatly. It is our tendency to measure the quality of a church by its packaging. The most evident application of this danger is in the electronic church. It has had a tremendous influence on Christians. However, this trend is visible in the local church as well. We have all fallen prey to this evil.

When the electronic church first started to appear on our national airwaves, I thought it was a good idea. It allowed us to reach millions of people with the gospel message. Additionally, it provided a worship service for shut-ins. The packaging was good, and the electronic church grew rapidly. However, as the church developed over the years, it has become apparent there are four evils which have arisen.

First: Leaders start out on a good course, but soon fall prey to pride and greed. They constantly have to grow bigger. Their appetite for more stations and funds is unsatiable.

Second: It has provided a fertile ground for "false prophets" preaching a message that sounds scriptural to those lacking in-depth Bible knowledge. Thousands are being deceived.

Third: Vast sums of money are going into production facilities and the pockets of station owners which could be better used to feed, clothe, and shelter those in need. These monies are being diverted from the local church which has great needs and proper oversight on their use.

Fourth: Leaders in the electronic church have attracted the attention of the news media. Problems which should be dealt with in the church are exposed to national publicity. The name of Christ is besmirched, as we have seen in recent years.

Unfortunately, most Christians look at the packaging and not at the substance of this type of church. They readily give of their funds for every purpose imaginable. There are no published statements of receipt and expenditure. Accountability for the actions of its leaders is non-existent, as long as they are able to avoid the national media attention. The church looks good on the outside, but it lacks the sweetness of good corn on the inside.

Moving to Florida, we started a search for a church in an area well blessed with churches. It proved to be a very disheartening affair. Invariably, after visiting a church, we would be paid a visit from someone on the calling committee. They would tell us about how many members were on the rolls, how fast they were growing, all of the activities they had going, and what a fine preacher the pastor was. Never once did we hear how much time they spent in prayer, fasting and weeping before the Lord.

The churches had become very program oriented. In the process, they had forgotten their prime calling--getting people to fight a spiritual warfare by growing in holiness. The church was packaging itself in a way the world would find attractive. Nevertheless, an active church doesn't make a good church. Its not the packaging, but what's inside the members that really counts.

John and Paul were concerned about this tendency to accept the packaging instead of the real product. The early church was just as guilty as we are.

In John's case, it was the willingness of an individual to house and send on their way, anyone claiming to be a messenger of God. It sounds like an old-time example of the electronic church. These messengers were benefitting from the funds given by a Christian who have no idea of the danger of their message, or how the funds were used. Souls were being deceived.

In Paul's case, the church was readily accepting worldly ideas as their standard of conduct. They would allow anything to develop within the church. If it sounded good, it must be good. They were interested in attracting as many members as possible. Both writers urged their readers to get back to the basics. It's the gospel message, not the packaging that counts.

Jesus, in the Sermon On The Mount, gave us the ground rules for the type of church He is seeking. It consists of eight controlling attitudes which must make up a kingdom citizen's life. These eight attitudes are: poor in spirit, mourning, meekness, hungering and thirsting for righteousness, merciful, pure in heart, peacemakers, and a willingness to suffer persecution for the sake of righteousness. How sadly lacking they are in the lives of most saints. We should spend time learning what these attitudes mean and how to acquire them. It would please our Savior greatly.

Jesus is really not concerned about how we package our Christianity. He wants a sweetness on the inside. Attractive ears of corn do not make a very delightful offering to the Lord. They may be closer to field corn rather than the real thing. He wants the best. He wants true sweet corn. May we seek that sweetness, and present ourselves as an acceptable sacrifice.

Father: We confess our sins of readily accepting the package without examining the substance. Some of us may have unwittingly helped spread messages not representative of the real product. We packaged it attractively, but there was a sweetness lacking. This is also true of our own lives. Too often we package ourselves in fine dress, makeup, jewelry, and community position. Help us to realize we are as blah as field corn. May we start today to acquire the sweetness of the real product. We ask it in Jesus' name and for His glory. Amen.

DAY 24
EGGPLANTS NEED WARM FEET

And let us consider one another to provoke unto love and to good works: Not forsaking the assembling of ourselves together, as the manner of some is; but exhorting one another: and so much the more, as ye see the day approaching. (Hebrews 10:24-25)

For it is impossible for those who were once enlightened....If they fall away, to renew them again unto repentance;
(Hebrews 6:4a, 6a)

Thought for the day:
Eggplants have to have warm feet in order to grow. Christians require the same condition. Proper warming will result in a bumper crop.

Loretta and I went out calling for our church. We were contacting members whose names were on the rolls, but never attended any of the services. We had hoped to encourage them to once again consider regular church attendance. The excuses we received were interesting. They showed how little interest some people have in the condition of their soul. We received the following comments. Enclosed in brackets, are the unspoken comments I would have liked to make.

"We only have one car." [Ever try walking?]

"Sunday mornings is the only time we get to sleep." [Nighttime is the usual time.]

"We used to come all the time and even had a youth group." [Don't you think your pew will grow cold?]

"I work all week!" [Doesn't everyone. Do you want a medal?]

"We have a picnic every Sunday and the tables fill up quickly. I have to get there by 10:30 in order to reserve a table." [Why not take a blanket and sit on the ground, the ants get hungry.]

The alibis would be humorous if they weren't so tragic. As the writer of Hebrews pointed out, once someone falls away, it is impossible to renew them again.

One year while living up north, I decided to plant a vegetable I had never grown before -- an eggplant. I love to eat them. Loretta makes the best eggplant parmesan, I have ever tasted. I could eat it "until the cows come home." I went to the nursery and purchased six plants. In late May they were set out, fertilized and watered. They grew very slowly. Finally, they budded and soon set their fruit. I could hardly wait until it would be time to harvest them. When the time came, I was very disappointed! My eggplants were the size of large eggs.

Failing to produce a satisfactory crop, I obeyed the old adage, "When everything else fails, read the instructions." I got out my garden books and read how eggplants like to have warm feet.

Undaunted, the next spring with six more plants in hand, I ventured out to the garden to try again. However, this time I proceeded a little differently. I took out a dark plastic garbage bag and laid it on the ground. I cut slits into it and planted the eggplants in the slits. The outcome was significant. The plants grew rapidly, and by harvest time I had eight full-size eggplants. Loretta was kept busy!

There always has to be the right climate for plants to grow properly. The same is true for new members to the faith. As a result, individually and corporately, we have a responsibility to provide a warm place for people to come, so they won't grow cold. Equally important, the individual has to make a commitment to keep his toes warm, so he will grow.

For some reason, God's frozen chosen really freeze up in their pews. They cannot smile, sing heartily, stay awake, and greet newcomers. Sometimes when I have been preaching, or just visiting another church, I was afraid the whole congregation had gone comatose. They just sat there staring. Any visitors would not have been impressed. There was no warmth in the congregation. Joy and a sense of praise was not forthcoming, either by mouth or facial expression.

I have read that one of the great leaders of India, Ghandi, attended church in London for a while. When asked why he never became a Christian, he replied that he didn't believe Christians really believed in their religion. They talked about joy, but their faces didn't show it. I have often wondered how many people we fail to win to the faith because we don't reflect the message of the gospel. Can you imagine the impact for Christ Ghandi could have made in India had he seen the London Christians enjoying their faith? Their action cost Christ more than one soul!

New Christians need to be made warm. Greetings should be given and friendships attempted. Gently, but persistently, they should be encouraged to attend church regularly, get involved with a Bible study, and participate in prayer meetings. Special emphasis should be made to call in their homes on a regular basis to make sure they feel welcome, and to let them know we really care for them. The right environment will go a long way to helping them grow rapidly.

However, our efforts should not extend only to the new

Christians. Long-time saints can become overworked or made to feel like they are excess baggage. Many a plant in my garden has shown great growth, but never produced as abundantly as it should have. For some reason, conditions were not proper. Let us not make the same mistake with long-time saints. They still need to be nurtured and brought to full fruition.

Individually, a Christian has to make a commitment to warming his or her toes. While Bible studies, prayer meetings and a warm congregation all help, unless a commitment is made they will not produce the intended results. Jesus, Paul, and Peter have given us a three step approach to make sure we stay toasty warm.

Jesus tells us never to look back. For some reason, humans have a tendency to always look back and remember the good times while forgetting the bad times. The allure to go back grows stronger as the bad fades from memory and the good old days become fonder. Soon we slip back into old ways, with old friends. Our faith grows cool and without even knowing it, we fall away from the church. Having come to Christ, there is only one way to go -- forward with Jesus. Anything else may put out our fire.

Paul tells us to look at the goal we want to attain. Heaven with an eternity of peace and joy must always be kept in our sights. A runner in a race doesn't stop to look back to see how far he has come from the starting blocks. Rather, his eyes are firmly fixed on the finish line, and He gives his all to achieve the goal. Why should we do less. Runners are only running for a medal. We are running for eternal bliss. After death, their medal will be melted down or thrown out. Our prize will be just beginning. Let us fix our eyes firmly on the goal.

Peter tells us to practice our Christianity. The more we apply the truths of the gospel, the more real they become. Our faith becomes rock solid, and we will not forget we have been purged from our sins. Our eyes will become better focused on what lies ahead, and we will become more diligent in making our calling and election sure. Peter promises us, if we do practice our Christianity, we will never fall.

The eggplants needed warmth to produce properly. We need to provide a proper environment for the Christian by offering warm loving relationships. They need to keep their toes warm by not looking back, keeping their eye on the goal, and practicing real Christian attitudes. Given the right conditions, I had plenty of eggplants to enjoy. Christ will have plenty of Souls to enjoy, if the right environment exists.

Father, help us to realize the importance of a proper atmosphere for Christian growth. Individually, ever keep before us the need to keep going forward, putting our eye on the goal, and daily practicing our faith. We ask it in Jesus' name. Amen.

DAY 25
WEEDS CAN BE VERY SNEAKY

Beware of false prophets, which come to you in sheep's clothing, but inwardly they are ravening wolves. Ye shall know them by their fruits. (Matthew 7:15-16a)

For there are certain men crept in unawares, who were before of old ordained to this condemnation, ungodly men, turning the grace of our God into lasciviousness, and denying the only Lord God, and our Lord Jesus Christ. (Jude 4)

Thought for the day:
Weeds are tricky. They have cleverly devised ways of ensuring their existence and destructive abilities. False prophets are equally as clever.

In one of the previous day's readings, I wrote about a weed I experienced in upstate New York. It put out long, thin roots. Periodically along the root system, it would send up a new plant. I would pull out roots one to two feet long with several plants attached. But, the root was very thin, easily breaking off. As a consequence, one never got it all. Soon it started to sprout anew.

Moving to Florida, I experienced a weed with a similar characteristic. Its leaves were totally different, but method of propagation exactly the same. I have pulled roots up to three feet long with many little plants attached. There is one difference between this root and the one in New York State. It is relatively thick and doesn't break off easily. Pulling it, gives you a certain confidence you are getting the whole root system. At least, that is what I originally felt. It didn't take long for me to realize this plant grew back as rapidly as the one in New York.

Frequent weeding showed me how the plant was able to revitalize itself, even when it was missing large sections of its root. It was a very sneaky weed. It would mesh its roots with the roots of other plants. This intertwining guaranteed a part of the root would break off, allowing the plant to grow again.

False prophets are a very sneaky lot. They bear a lot of resemblance to this weed. Every writer of the New Testament letters warned their constituency against false prophets. Jude tells us they creep in unawares. John warns us to test the spirits. Peter tells us they are liars. Paul warns us they appear as ministers of light. They were very abundant then, they are abundant today. It is one weed we are incapable of destroying.

Jesus realized the danger they would represent to His followers. In the Sermon of the Mount, He called our attention to their danger. He placed upon us the responsibility to carefully weigh each person's actions, determining whether He was a true lamb, or a wolf in lamb's clothing. It isn't always easy.

False prophets come into a body of believers in a very sneaky manner. They don't enter wearing a neon sign flashing "False Prophet". Outwardly they appear to be a member of the flock. They fit in very comfortably, seem to know Scripture, pretend to worship Jesus. They are very charming and friendly.

How are we ever to know what is the truth and what isn't? Is there a way to spot a false prophet? Can we be sure our ministers and teachers are men of God? These are questions we must ask ourselves if we are going to be on guard against this ever present danger. It is our responsibility to protect ourselves and to defend the faith for future generations. It is a task we have not been concerned enough about.

The starting point is the Bible. We have to be thoroughly knowledgeable about its teachings. However, this is not always the easiest or fastest way to gain knowledge. The Bible can be hard to understand for several reasons.

First: The writers follow eastern type of thinking. It is not always easy for westerners to follow their logic.

Second: They were writing using the perspective and life styles of their day. We are not totally knowledgeable in these things and find it difficult to relate what they say to the message they are trying to convey.

Third: The Bible has to have Scripture matched against Scripture, in order to obtain a balanced understanding of all facets of the subject. It is a large book and takes years to totally digest.

These problems are formidable, but they should not stop us from proceeding with a systematic reading and study of the Bible. In time, we will develop the knowledge we need. It will be invaluable in assisting us to identify false prophets.

A second source of help is the Holy Spirit. John says we do not need to have men teach us. As we are anointed by the Holy Spirit, He will guide us into all truth. In fact, this is one of the prime ministries of the Holy Spirit. Jesus calls Him the Spirit of truth. Seeking His help in prayer should be a prime concern of each saint.

The Holy Spirit will give us a sense something is wrong when a false prophet appears in our midst. We may not know exactly what the problem is, but we will be given an uneasy feeling when the wolf is present. Additionally, the Spirit will guide us to other men of God who will assist us. Furthermore, if we will seek the Spirit's help as we read the Bible, we will be given insights into passages and how they relate to the individual in question.

The problem we have in utilizing the direction and guidance of the Holy Spirit is our tendency to have a closed mind. We might like a person who is a false prophet. After all, they are cleverly disguised. Therefore, we will ignore the prodding of the Spirit. Even when we sense something is wrong, we are more apt to blame it on innumerable other things, rather than carefully seek the Spirit's guidance in the matter.

Perhaps the easiest and plainest way to detect a false prophet is through our eyes. Even though the neon sign is missing, there will be trail markers plainly visible. Keeping our eyes posted for the following two signs will quickly help us to detect those individuals we are to avoid.

First: Study the fruit a person bears. A false prophet will manipulate things so there is never peace and harmony in the body of believers. They either will start the trouble, or they will twist things in a fashion which prevents a complete solution and keeps the turmoil boiling.

Second: Notice how they use Scripture. Most false prophets will twist things just a little bit. It sounds good, but it isn't exactly the way the Bible records it. Other false prophets will tend to base their whole teaching around a few obscure passages, using these to destroy the major doctrines. Still others will only teach one subject. They never present a balanced viewpoint.

The unfortunate part is the long term problems created by these wolves. Their roots seem to intertwine and break off in a congregation, much like a weed. Even after a false prophet has been properly dealt with, their destructive tendencies will still adhere and surface in the lives of some members. Constant weeding and an ever watchful eye are necessary. At the first appearance of new growth, it must be quickly pulled. If we fail in our duties, heresy may destroy the faith.

Utilizing the Bible, seeking the help of the Holy Spirit, and keeping our eyes open will help us to avoid falling prey to these ravening wolves. While dangerous, they can be recognized and avoided. We will never rid ourselves of this menace. We can keep it under control, protecting our garden of faith, and preserving it for future generations. Let us keep our weeding tools readily available and in use..

Father, Help us at all times to be aware of the possibility of false prophets in our midst. Give us the discernment necessary for quick detection when they appear. Protect us and be our fortress and guide. For Jesus' sake we pray. Amen.

DAY 26
GARNERING SHEAVES IS HARD WORK

So she gleaned in the field until even, and beat out that she had gleaned: and it was about an ephah of barley.
(Ruth 2:17)

Therefore, my beloved brethren, be ye stedfast, unmoveable, always abounding in the work of the Lord, forasmuch as ye know that your labour is not in vain in the Lord. (I Corinthians 15:58)

Thought for the day:
Hard work often goes unnoticed by our fellow man. Nevertheless, the Ruler of the Universe has seen, and our reward will be in proportion to our faithfulness.

One summer, when I was about fifteen, I was helping my grandfather on his farm. Just prior to school starting, the corn had matured and was ready to be made into silage. He gave me a sickle and drove me to the middle of the corn patch bordering on a path across the meadow. Using a sickle, I was to cut down three rows of corn. This would allow the tractor and harvester to come down the middle of the field and save time in the reaping process.

It really didn't look like too tough of a job. Just swing the sickle, catch the stalk, and put it in a pile. However, the first swing of the sickle convinced me otherwise. It only penetrated the corn stalk about a third of the way. I had to yank on it several times to get it through the stalk. It was not a snap job.

When noon came, my grandfather came to pick me up for lunch. I had worked about three hours. Sweat was running down my brow into my eyes, my arms and back ached, and I had multiple blisters on each hand. I was beat, and only one-half way through the corn field. Then came the cruelest blow of all. The first words out of my grandfather's mouth was, "Is this all you got done?" I was crushed. I knew I had worked extremely hard and given it my all.

Later in life, I had another experience which again revealed to me the amount of effort required to harvest crops. I had a vegetable garden and the crop was excellent. Normally, Loretta and I would work together in preparing the vegetables for freezing and canning. However, this year she was unable to assist me due to illness. I would go out to the garden at the first crack of dawn and harvest the crop. The vegetables were taken into the house, washed, culled, and prepared for blanching. After blanching, they were packed into freezer bags and frozen. Normally, several hours were spent on each vegetable, prior to putting it in the freezer for the coming winter. It was tiring work, doing it all alone.

As a result of those two experiences, I have a great appreciation for the labor Ruth performed in gleaning the fields in order to provide for her mother-in-law and herself.

Old Testament law required the farmers to leave some of their crop along the borders for the poor. God wanted the poor to have the opportunity to provide for themselves by reaping these patches and gleaning the fields for dropped stalks of wheat and barley. The poor not only were able to eat, but they gained some self-respect by being able to provide for their family.

Ruth had lost her husband and was living with her

mother-in-law Naomi, also a widow. Times were tough for those two. Ruth undertook the task of trying to provide food for them. She would go out to the fields to glean at harvest time. Going along the patches left along the edges and corners of fields and using her sickle she would harvest sheaves of grain. If those areas had already been harvested by other poor, she would walk behind the reapers, and pick up any dropped stalks. It was hard, back breaking work.

The passage quoted above says she worked from dawn to dusk. Then she had to beat the seeds off of the stalk, toss them into the wind to winnow the chaff from the seed, and gather the seed into a basket before her labors were done. On one particular day she was especially fortunate. Boaz, the owner of the field, had ordered his reapers to occasionally drop a whole handful of stalks for Ruth to glean. As a result, by the time she had completed her labors, she had harvested slightly over a bushel of grain for Naomi and herself. Her labor had not been in vain.

Later, Ruth, a gentile, married Boaz. Through their descendants came King David and eventually the Lord Jesus. Her devotion to her mother-in-law, and her labors to provide food for their daily livelihood were honored by God. The record of her faithfulness has been recorded and preserved by the Holy Spirit for thousands of years.

Ruth provides an excellent source of encouragement for us. We serve a great God. Nothing we do ever goes unrewarded. God repays our efforts many times over, just as He did Ruth.

It may not always be what we do in church that counts the most. For Ruth, it was the laborious task of providing food in a faithful manner which caused God to highly esteem her in His Word.

For Rahab, it was hiding the spies in Jericho. Nevertheless, God saw the tenderness of their heart and their faithfulness to others. He honored both of them.

Sometimes, we have the tendency to think our actions and service toward others goes unnoticed. While this may be true from the human standpoint, it never is from the spiritual standpoint. God always sees and rewards. We can always be assured our labors are not in vain. Whether it is teaching Sunday School, being a deacon, serving on the kitchen committee, being the sexton of the church, or helping a friend, God rewards the activity.

God is not concerned so much with the type of activity we perform for Him, as He is with the way we perform the activity. He is looking for people who are faithful, willing to work hard, and will perform their duties without grumbling or vain-glorying. Ruth willingly gave of herself, and God honored her. God is looking for the same type of person today, and will reward accordingly.

Another lesson to be learned from Ruth is her willingness to hang in there hour after hour. It was hard work, with the sun beating down on her. She was bent over most of the time, picking up a stalk here and there. Occasionally she would have to swing her sickle to cut the stalk. After she had reaped all day, she beat and winnowed the grain. Ruth could have taken it home to Naomi and asked her to do her part in getting the grain ready for use. Instead, she continued to work until the job was complete.

How often we give up before the job is complete. We get discouraged, or we find the task too time consuming. It becomes all too easy for us to call the pastor and tell him we can't do it anymore. If the task is not completed, we expect others to come along and complete it for us. Our service is more one of convenience than one of true faithfulness.

Unfortunately, victory might have been just around the corner. For Ruth, her victory was in finding a husband capable of loving her and providing for her and Naomi. She had no idea God would honor her by allowing her to be an ancestor for Jesus. She hung in there and reaped a great reward. May we learn from her example.

That early experience in the corn field taught me not to always expect praise, regardless of how hard I may have worked. I had the personal satisfaction of knowing I had given it my all. My blisters, aching arms and back convinced me I could not have done any more than I did. It was a good feeling.

Freezing and canning the vegetables by myself helped me to appreciate how much it means to have others pitch in and help. I missed the help of my wife. I really could have used her assistance. It was the Lord's way of reminding of the necessity to always be ready to help others in their tasks. Rather than letting them burn themselves out going it alone, we should be ready to pitch in and help them achieve the victory.

Father, We thank you for the example of Ruth. Her dedication to duty was commendable. You rewarded her accordingly. May we be as faithful. Help us to always remember, our labors will not be in vain. We ask it in Jesus' name. Amen.

DAY 27
BLACKBERRY THORNS HURT

From the end of the earth will I cry unto thee, when my heart is overwhelmed: lead me to the rock that is higher than I.
(Psalms 61:2)

Beloved, think it not strange concerning the fiery trial which is to try you, as though some strange thing happened unto you: (I Peter 4:12)

Thought for the day:
Blackberry thorns have to be endured if we are to pick this delectable fruit. The fruits of a deep faith in Christ are likewise obtained as we bear the thorns of life.

As a young boy, I didn't realize how fortunate I was to grow up in the country. The "city kids" seemed to have all the fun. They were always going to each other's house, playing ball, and never seemed to work. On the other hand, the farm was work, work, and loneliness. Now, as I look back on those years, I can see how they instilled within me a real appreciation for all God does for us. Of course, at the time, I didn't know him. We never attended church or read the Bible. Still God was preparing me to understand some of His greatest lessons in the simplest of situations.

When August rolled around, it was time for Dad and me to head for the woods to pick blackberries. I have to admit, I didn't like picking them and would have skipped out of the task if I could have found a good excuse. Even though I enjoyed the woods, and occasionally a handful of fresh berries, it was hot, tiring work.

We would put on heavy long sleeved shirts to protect our arms, and wear boots to protect our legs from the briars. It always seemed like the best berries were in the thickest part of the bramble patch, and a lot of dead brambles had to be trampled under foot to get to them. Even with all the protection, our hands, face and body would get scratched. Those scratches would sting for several days afterward.

We carried a large twelve quart pail and two small ones. The small ones we hung on our belts in order to keep our hands free to pick berries and move the sharp briars out of the way. As the small pails became full, they were emptied into the big pail. When the big pail was heaped full to compensate for any settling, we would fill our small pails one more time before heading home. The berries in the big pail always went into cans or jam for winter. The smaller pails were our immediate reward for the labor.

I used to sit down with a large bowl of blackberries, sprinkled with sugar and covered with fresh milk. There were always several slices of bread with butter sitting beside the bowl. A whole meal was made out of those fresh blackberries. It made the scratched arms, tired legs, and lost play-time well worth the effort. It also taught me a valuable lesson about life, and more importantly about my spiritual life which was to come later.

Good things require some hardship. Most of us are not born with a silver spoon in our mouth. We work hard, try to pay our bills on time, and over our working years attempt to accumulate enough for retirement and a few years of enjoyment on planet earth. When we finally retire, we look back over those years of toil and realize it was well worth it. We understand our struggles were all part of life, and make the results taste even sweeter.

Those years on the farm instilled me with a work ethic. I came to understand nothing is easy in this world. If gain is to be made, it could only be accomplished through hard work. The farm we had was a small one, and not the source of any direct income. It did make us somewhat self-sufficient as we raised a large portion of food supply. In addition we often gathered from the fields and woods. Blackberries, wild strawberries, blueberries, apples, and nuts were readily available to supplement our own production of dairy products, meat and vegetables. Dad and Mom worked at jobs, so I was expected to carry a large portion of the daily gardening and farm chores. It taught me hard work was a vital and necessary part of life.

The Christian life requires the same type of work ethic. While it is needed in the various activities of our churches, it is needed even more in our private growth. Only as we grow personally are we able to become truly productive in the church's activities. Those activities are blessed by God only when they are performed with the right Christian attitudes and in accordance with His Word. It is in the individual spiritual training ground where the going gets really rough.

God the master teacher often gives us a bed of roses complete with the stems. We may like the flowers, but the thorns prick and scratch just as badly as those blackberry brambles. It is His way of getting us to: (1) appreciate the roses, (2) get back into line, (3) grow spiritually.

Trying to work our way to heaven would place a tremendous burden upon us. We would be laboring under bondage to a whole set of rules, while never being sure we had properly covered every base. Guilt and concern would prevent any type of peace from flooding our soul.

We enjoy the relief of knowing we are free from the consequences of our sins. However, we sometimes are not very appreciative of this freedom. We forget the one who made it all possible. As a result our relationship with Christ becomes more a recognition of what He did, rather than a personal on-going abiding in His presence. It is at those times, God sends some briars to prick us and make us more appreciative. He is making us aware we are leaving Christ out of life. We need to re-focus our directions and smell the sweetness of the Rose of Sharon.

There are other times when we are disobedient either through acts of commission or omission. When these times occur, God sends some thorns our way to make us to re-examine our lives and find out what is the cause of our problems. Due to our stubbornness, the bramble patch can get pretty big. There may be a lot of thorns we have to endure before we get to the heart of the problem.

Many times the outward problems we are experiencing are the result of inward attitudes we didn't know existed. Only as problems and pressures are brought to bear, do we begin to root out those thorny attitudes and trample them underfoot. Real Christian growth most often occurs while in the middle of the briar patch. Finally, after enough briar scratches, we begin to wake up. We see our sins and understand the reason for the thorns. We humbly kneel before God seeking His forgiveness. Soon the big berries of renewal come into view, and we can sit down and enjoy the results.

We may be walking on a spiritual high, enjoying a daily abiding presence with Christ, while living a righteous life. All of a sudden we find ourselves going through a thorn patch. We become confused and begin to wonder what is happening. All sorts of questions begin to rush through our minds. "Where am I sinning?" "Why doesn't God care about me any more?" "Is there really a God, or have I been deluded?" The questions go on and on.

Many times it is God just taking us deeper into our faith. He wants to bring us to the point where we have a perfect confidence in Him, willingly accepting everything He commands. By creating doubts, He causes us to seek for answers. In the end, we see His hand behind it all. Our assurance in His watchful care is strengthened. We surrender a little more of our lives to Him. Our increased faith has brought us into a deeper Christian walk.

Often times I have wished there were other ways of growing in greater appreciation of Christ, walking a more righteous life, and experiencing a deeper faith, other than experiencing the briar patches of life. It is at those times, I like to remember my days in the blackberry patch. The thorns smarted, but the end result was well worth the effort. I get my eyes off the problem and look for the end results. It makes the trial easier.

Father, thank you for the thorns of life. I know it is part of your lessons in faith, bringing me into a deeper relationship with you. I look forward to the berries it will produce. I praise you in Jesus' name. Amen.

DAY 28
TRY AND GET THE LAST WEED

Children, obey your parents in the Lord: for this is right. Honour thy father and mother; which is the first commandment with promise; That it may be well with thee, and thou.
(Ephesians 6:1-3)

Because it is written, Be ye holy; for I am holy.
(I Peter 1:16)

Thought for the day:
We can weed until our hearts are content, and the next day we'll find another weed. Growing in righteousness is very similar: there is always one more weed sin to pull. Lessons learned in childhood will help us in pulling those weeds.

I have been gardening ever since I can remember. As a little boy, I was constantly with my parents as they worked in the garden. At first I assisted them by picking up stones and asking a million questions. As I grew older, I was given a stick a foot long and shown how to plant five kernels of corn, spaced apart by the length of the stick. When I asked why five kernels, the reply was, "One for the crow, one to die, and three to grow". As I finished a row, Dad would cover it with the hoe. Next I was given a six inch stick and shown how to plant onion bulbs with the roots down.

When I got to the age of six or seven, I was given a row in the garden as my very own. I planted several different vegetables in a very short row, but I looked forward to reaping a bountiful harvest just the same. Also, I was put in charge of the squash and pumpkin plants to make sure they were weeded, and kept from running into the meadow where they would have been destroyed during haying.

By the time I was a teenager, the garden, once it was planted, became my prime responsibility. I was expected to weed, cultivate, and hoe the rows. I'm afraid my parents had to be on my back quite a bit, just to get the minimum amount of gardening done. I had a million other things I could find to do, mainly play.

There was one thing I was faithful at -- debugging. We never used insecticide on our garden. As part of my daily duties I had to make sure the worms and bugs were not eating up the garden, especially the potatoes. Every morning I would go out to the potato patch and pick the potato bugs. I had a coffee can with a little kerosene in the bottom. The bugs would be picked off the leaf and dropped into the kerosene. I would look under the leaves for their cluster of yellow eggs. When they were found, they would be crushed between two stones. I also kept careful guard over the other vegetables, but they never posed the challenge the potato bugs did. Those little monsters seemed to materialize out of thin air. We did have a healthy garden, albeit a weedy one at times.

The summer I was sixteen, I became determined to have the nicest looking garden my parents had ever seen. Every morning for two hours or three hours, I would go down the rows of plants pulling weeds. Then I would push a hand cultivator down the middle of the rows. This was followed by taking a hoe and pulling the dirt up around the plants. The garden was beautiful and absolutely weed free. I felt a real sense of accomplishment.

One evening when Dad came home from work, I had to take him out and show him the results of my labor. My chest was bursting with pride. We went around the barn, and I pointed out how beautiful and weed free the garden was. Then I looked between a row of beets and there right in the middle of a row as healthy as could be was a weed about nine inches high. To this day, I am convinced it sprang up in a couple of hours. I hung my head and went over and pulled it out. I was totally embarrassed, ashamed, and completely convinced my labors had all been in vain. My father's remark didn't help to relieve my humility. He said, "It doesn't look too bad." I had worked hard, and one lousy weed had destroyed it all.

Trying to grow in righteousness and live a sinless life is a lot like pulling weeds in the garden. No matter how much we weed sin out of our lives, a new giant weed appears, almost over night. Sometimes, I get terribly frustrated with myself. I try so hard to live a life pleasing to Jesus, yet my garden seems to grow weeds better than it grows fruit. When they make their appearance, I am just as totally embarrassed, ashamed, and convinced my labors are all in vain, as I was that day in the garden showing off to Dad. I'm glad I know a Savior who is forgiving and patient. Were He not, I'm sure I would have been discarded on the scrap heap long ago. Those weeds can sure teach one humility.

While my family was not a church going family, (I was the first one to accept Christ), they did install in me the importance of hard work, sense of duty, obedience, and responsibility for my actions. Later, these qualities carried over into my religious life. They provide the motivation to keep on growing in righteousness. Rather than giving up as sin makes its appearance, I do like I did with that one weed. I hang my head in humility and go to work to pull it out.

Now I know my entrance in heaven doesn't depend upon having all the weeds pulled. However, I do want to please Jesus and show Him my gratitude for dying for my sins. The best way I know how to do that is by diligently weeding my life of those things which are wrong. The job will never be finished, until I get to Heaven, but Jesus looks on the nature of my heart, sees the outward attempts, and knows I love Him and am trying to please. I suspect He may even think, "It doesn't look too bad" at times. At least, until the next giant weed stands erect and healthy between the virtues I have grown.

We parents should never overlook the importance of developing a child's virtues through work. They will stand the child in good stead all through life. Part of the problems we face with our youth today is a result of their never having learned any sense of duty, obedience and responsibility. Work hasn't been a part of their lives. They have learned to be couch-potatoes and expect to be handed the world on a silver tray. Many are coming out of school with a diploma, unable to read, write or do simple math.

Just two days ago, my wife went into the bank, gave the teller a twenty dollar bill, asked for five dollars in dimes and two dollars in nickels. The teller had to use a calculator to determine she owed Loretta thirteen dollars in bills to balance the transaction. Obviously during her school years she had never been forced to apply herself. I wonder what her parents were doing.

We Christian parents have even more reason to instill within our children the need to work hard and accept responsibility for their actions. It will help them to come to a saving knowledge of Christ and motivate them to grow in righteousness. While we may have to get on their backs to force them to action, in the later years they will appreciate the qualities we have instilled in them. Let us take our duties seriously and keep involved in giving our children virtues that can make a difference in adulthood. They will thank us in the end.

I didn't always please my parents, but they didn't give up on me. They forced me to accept responsibility for my actions. Today, I appreciate their efforts. I am laboring diligently to grow in righteousness, knowing I have a responsibility to live a life pleasing to my Savior. He died for me, so it is the least I can do in return for Him. The weeds will go on being pulled, because my parents taught me to work hard, accept responsibility, and not give up. They are good virtues to start life with.

The real reward for applying those qualities will be realized when I stand before the Savior and hear him say, "Well done thou good and faithful servant." It will be doubly rewarding when we hear Him say it to our children, because we instilled them with the virtues that carried us through life. May we each renew our efforts in training our children the benefits of hard work. It will never fail them in their secular life; it will benefit them greatly in their spiritual life.

Father, we thank You for Your Son. He means so very much to us, and we do want to please Him by demonstrating to Him our desire to grow in righteousness. May we ever apply the principles of hard work, sense of duty, obedience, and responsibility for our actions in all we do to please Him. We ask it in His name. Amen.

DAY 29
WEEDING IS LONELY WORK

Think not that I am come to send peace on the earth: I came not to send peace, but a sword. For I am come to set a man at variance against his father, and the daughter against her mother, and the daughter in law against her mother in law. And a man's foes shall be they of his own household.
(Matthew 10:34-36)

Do thy diligence to come shortly unto me: For Demas hath forsaken me, having loved this present world, and is departed unto Thessalonica;...Only Luke is with me.
(II Timothy 4:9-10a, 11a)

Thought for the day:
People never volunteer to help a gardener weed. Yet, they appreciate the beauty of the garden. Weeding sin from our lives can be lonely work, however, the Trinity will appreciate the beauty and reward us accordingly.

There is one thing I have learned during my years of gardening: weeding is lonely work. I have spent hundreds of hours pulling weeds, and I can't think of a single time when any of my family or neighbors have stopped by and said, "Can I help you?" However, as soon as I put away the tools, they seem to materialize out of thin air with comments about how nice the garden looks.

I have used this tendency to my advantage. Many times,

if I want to get away for some peace and quiet, I slip into my gardening rags, grab the weed pail, and start to weed. Instantly, I have peace and quiet.

It is amazing how much relaxation one can experience while pulling weeds. I can get so involved with weeds, my problems are pushed into the background. Nothing bothers me except where to find the next weed and how to get all of its roots. It's as though I had vanished into another world. Two or three hours can slip rapidly by. When I stop, there is a refreshing to my soul. The world is put into proper perspective.

Something else often happens when I am weeding. The Holy Spirit starts to speak to me about eternal truths. All of a sudden, I will begin to contemplate how a particular weed reveals something about sin, or I will recall some event from a past gardening experience and catch an insight into God's great plan. Much of this book is the result of ideas I've garnered while pulling weeds. The peace and solitude allows my spirit to connect with the Holy Spirit in an intimate way. Through gardening, I am able to open myself up to His quiet direction. Undoubtedly, God knew it would affect people that way, and has blessed us with a desire to have a "green thumb".

Living a life for the Savior by growing in righteousness is also lonely work. The harder one works at ridding oneself of sin, spending more time in prayer, studying the Bible, and praising Jesus, the more abandoned one becomes. It's not that everyone has gone away, they just are staying out of the way. However, just commit a sin, and they are right there telling you what a terrible thing you did. People don't want to help you any more than they want to help weed the garden. Nevertheless, they have you under their scrutiny and are always ready to comment on the job you are doing.

Jesus said it would be like that. When one comes totally to Him, there is a separation that occurs. We may not want it to happen, but others will make it occur. Basically, I think there are two reasons for this.

First: They are too lazy to weed their own garden. They know they have sin and are not living for Jesus, but they don't want to put forth the effort to correct the problem. They wouldn't want to divorce themselves from the TV set for an hour of prayer. Some stupid article in a magazine will command more of their attention than a chapter in the Bible. Righteousness, like weeding, takes work. They would rather enjoy themselves.

Second: They like their weeds. It doesn't bother their conscience at all, for they love the things of the world more than they love Jesus. Why give up a favorite sin, it's so much "fun". Disregard the emptiness, struggles, and lack of peace it causes in their life. They don't see the connection between the two.

When I read the above passage from Timothy, I feel the hurt Paul was feeling. He was in prison, and everybody had left him. Some apparently went to other mission fields or churches. But Demas had gone back into the world. He couldn't give up the world. He preferred weeds to fruitfulness. Paul was feeling the pain of seeing a fellow worker desert the cause of Christ and eternal bliss for the enjoyment of a few hours of what the world could offer. You can just feel the hurt coming through in the few words Paul wrote.

Paul's commitment to Christ had cost him dearly. He had suffered all kinds of beatings, shipwrecks, imprisonment, mockery, and other perils. Nevertheless, Paul, through it all, kept weeding his garden and urging others to do the same.

Growing in righteousness was Paul's way of saying, "Thank you Jesus." He would not cheapen the death of the Savior by continuing to allow weeds to grow. The price paid for his salvation was high, and if he went on living his past life, Paul would have seen it as a disgrace and dishonoring of Jesus. Weeds are pulled to beautify a garden. Paul would pull weeds to beautify the work of Jesus.

Living in righteousness was lonely work for Paul. He traveled to many strange lands, preached the gospel facing great opposition, and then at a time in his life when he was under the sentence of death, a close worker deserts him for a garden of weeds. Yet, never once does he think it wasn't worth it. In fact, Paul felt very strongly in the opposite direction. He considered it the most important facet of life. It was so important he constantly called upon his readers to imitate him.

When we consider all that it cost him, and then read his call to walk in righteousness as he walked in righteousness, a person realizes Paul must have received tremendous spiritual benefits. It didn't provide much in this world as is evident from his life. But, it did provide a great deal of personal satisfaction, self worth, peace, joy, love, and harmony with the Trinity. These were infinitely more important than a few moments of ease. Weeding brought satisfaction to his soul.

Having realized the great benefits of a righteous walk, we can begin to understand even more deeply how it must have hurt Paul to see Demas go back into the world. He knew what Demas was giving up. The worldly joy of the moment would never bring the deep peace and satisfaction righteousness could give him. It would be fleeting, and in the end result in insecurity, trouble, and distress. It wasn't a very good deal.

I have personally experienced something similar to

Paul's experience. I witnessed a fellow worker in the Lord's work go back into the world. He had come out of gross sin, prospered in the Lord, had become a soul winner and a truly on-fire Christian. But then, the call of this world started to have its effect. Soon the life of righteousness became too difficult. He gave it up and went back to the weed patch.

Weeding is lonely difficult work. However, it does produce a garden of beauty, one admired by family and neighbors alike. Weeding our soul of all sin may not always be admired by our family or neighbors as it does bring about separation from them. However, and certainly infinitely more important, it wins the praise of the Holy Trinity. They come and take up their abode with the individual who has learned to overcome the weeds of the world. They bestow upon those individuals, the peace, joy, and love we are all seeking and only they can bestow. These qualities far exceed the fleeting joy of sin. They are to be desired above all else. May we understand its importance.

Father, please continue to impress upon us, Your people, the need to daily weed our lives of all sin. When You see people deserting us, draw closer to us. When temptation arises calling us back into the garden of weeds, show us anew the fruits of righteousness. May we please You with our lives. We ask it in Jesus' name. Amen.

DAY 30
AUTUMN IS A MATTER OF PERSPECTIVE

For me to live is Christ and to die is gain. For I am in a strait betwixt two, having a desire to depart, and to be with Christ; which is far better:
(Philippians 1:21, 23)

.And God shall wipe away all tears from their eyes; and there shall be no more death, neither sorrow, nor crying, neither shall there be any more pain: for the former things are passed away. And He that sat upon the throne said, Behold I make all things new. And he said unto me, Write: for these words are true and faithful.
(Revelation 21:4-5)

Thought for the day:
How we view the end of the growing season depends on the perspective we have regarding its meaning. Our spiritual life is also affected by perspective. Where our eyes are focused determines our every action.

It was late summer, and the days had started to take on the feel of fall. There was a certain quietness settling upon the earth. The sun had lost some of its warmth, and the mornings had a briskness to them. The birds' song had turned to a different tune as they started to gather in flocks for their trip south. Fall was definitely on its way.

This was even more apparent in my gardens. Most of the vegetables had been harvested. There still remained a few late tomatoes ripening on the vines, and a late planting of beans providing a few more meals. The rest of the garden was bare, with the plants assigned to the mulch pile. The flower beds were also experiencing a change. The mums were in bloom, the petunias were starting to look yellow, other plants had ceased blooming altogether. While the marigolds were still blossoming profusely, the beds lacked the vitality they possessed a month earlier.

One morning, I arose to a real chill in the air. Looking out the window at the lawn, it was evident Jack Frost had made the first fall visit to the area. That evening, on returning from work, Jack's work was evident. The marigolds' leaves hung down and were a dark ugly black color. The petunias, roses, and beans also gave evidence to the onset of fall. Their life cycle was complete.

Now would begin the work of preparing the flower beds for winter. The dead plants would be pulled, the roses and rhubarb would be banked with leaves to protect the roots. Permanent plants would be cut back. There would be leaves to rake, bird houses to take down, and bird feeders to set up. In a few short weeks there would be a deadness upon the earth.

Loretta and I have opposing views about fall. She hates the fall because everything is dying. It makes her feel very sad. She prefers to look forward to spring. The first crocuses pushing through the frozen earth, the tips of the tulips starting to appear bring her great joy. She sees the newness of life and it makes her feel alive and excited.

I enjoy the fall. The final burst of color in the northern forests reaches down into my soul. I can spend hours walking in the woods enjoying the color, watching the leaves float to earth on gentle breezes. There is a peace and serenity creeping over the land. The pleasantly warm days, the chill of the nights exhilarates my senses.

The reason Loretta and I have these opposing views lies in our perspective. She sees the deadness of the winter about to settle upon the earth. It will be a time void of color and excitement. A time when one feels the coldness, and easily develops cabin fever from staying inside to keep warm.

I don't discern the deadness. Rather I see a promise of a greater glory. The coloring of the trees speaks to me about the beauty awaiting us in Heaven. The pleasantness of the days reminds me of the peace and serenity God has in store for His saints. The excitement of the changing season tells me Heaven will be an exciting adventure. I love being outdoors viewing the splendor and feeling the change.

Perspective affects our Christian outlook as well. Where we have our eyes focused will determine to a great deal how we live our daily lives. If our eyes are focused on the day to day struggles to exist, our activity will reflect our focus. Our personal cares and concerns will be paramount in our thoughts. There will be unnecessary worry, a willingness to bend our ethics in order to claw our way up the corporate ladder, and lies will be easier to tell in order to make ourselves look good. Our whole tendency will be to act like the world. We are in the world, and we live by the world's standards.

However, if our eyes are fixed firmly on Heaven, we will reflect that focus. Knowing we will someday be spending eternity in Heaven, we will begin to prepare ourselves for our appearance before the King. Our desire is to hear Him say, "Well done thou good and faithful servant." We will work at growing in holiness, walking our talk in every action we take, while continually seeking His guidance and direction for every step. Acting as His servant, there will be found an abundance of time to do His work. Things of this earth will grow pale, and our objective becomes a true longing for His presence.

Perspective will also affect how we face death. Knowing where we are going and what awaits us should produce a calmness, perhaps even an longing for the time we will cross over the great divide. Fear and dread will be overcome. Satan's bondage will be completely broken, since the fear of death no longer controls our minds. We know where we are headed, and the expectation of it will fill our souls with a sense of excitement.

Paul had his eyes firmly fixed on the goal. His perspective was totally focused on standing in the presence of his Savior. He had come to the point in his life where he was longing to depart, in order to enter into the very presence of the one he loved and served so dearly. He wanted the peace, joy, and beauty Heaven offered.

Even though Paul wrote extensively about grace, condemning those who would try to work their way to heaven, he still would live life as though attaining Heaven depended on his every action. It wasn't so much He was afraid of falling away, but rather, Heaven was so fixed in his focus, he would not even risk the possibility of losing the goal. He would, therefore, face any danger, preach the gospel in far off lands, spend himself completely in his attempt to make the goal. He controlled his every action, bringing himself into total submission to God, lest he should somehow lose the prize set before him. What an admirable way to live.

We occasionally develop near-sightedness, and are unable to see the finish line. Therefore, we only run toward what we can see. Most of us will spend more time preparing for a few years of retirement than we will on spending eternity in heaven. Some of us are so near-sighted we can't even see retirement, just making it through tomorrow becomes our finish line. We need to get fitted with corrective lenses.

When frost starts to settle on the pumpkins, and our flower beds cease their blooming, each of us should stop and take stock of where our eyes are fixed. We need to re-establish our target, realigning our lives in order to ensure hitting the goal. This periodic eye examination will help us to put life into proper perspective. Those things helping to guarantee our entrance into heaven will become paramount, and the mundane will fade. Our perspective of heaven is a vital part of Christian growth.

Father, we confess we too often focus on the short term. As a result, our lives do not reflect our desires. We fail to run toward the goal of heaven. Change our perspective. Sharpen our focus on the beauty, joy, and excitement only heaven can provide. Help us to run toward the finish line. In Jesus's name. Amen.

INDEX OF BIBLE VERSES BY THE DAY

DAY 1
Genesis 2:7-9a

DAY 2
Genesis 3:17b, 18b, 19a

DAY 3
Genesis 2:9; 3:22-23

DAY 4
Genesis 2:17; 3:4-5

DAY 5
Genesis 2:15

DAY 6
Psalms 62:3

DAY 7
Genesis 3:17-19a
Job 31:38-40a

DAY 8
Genesis 1:26
Ephesians 1:4

DAY 9
Genesis 3:6

DAY 10
Proverbs 27:6a
Galatians 6:1, 3

DAY 11
Deuteronomy 20:16-17a, 18
Judges 2:12

DAY 12
Proverbs 22:6
I Thessalonians 4:1
I Peter 2:21, 24a

DAY 13
John 15:2

DAY 14
Hebrews 12:4; 12-13

DAY 15
Genesis 4:9b
I Corinthians 6:12

DAY 16
Leviticus 20:24
II Corinthians 6:17-18

DAY 17
Romans 6:6

DAY 18
Romans 1:19-20

DAY 19
Luke 3:9

BIBLE VERSES BY THE BOOK

Genesis 1:11-12; 26; 2:7-9, 15, 17; 3:4-6, 17-19a, 22-23; 4:9b
Leviticus 20:24
Deuteronomy 20:16-17a,18
Judges 2:12
Ruth 2:17

Job 31:38-40a
Psalms 61:2; 62:3
Proverbs 22:6; 27:6a
Matthew 7:15-16a; 10:34-36
Luke 3:9

John 15:2
Romans 1:19-20; 6:6
I Corinthians 6:12; 15:58
II Corinthians 6:17-18
Galatians 6:1, 3

Ephesians 1:4; 6:1-3
Philippians 1:21, 23; 3:17-18
Colossians 2:8
I Thessalonians 4:1
II Timothy 1:6; 4:9-10a, 11a

Hebrews 6:4a, 6a; 10:24-25; 12:4; 12-13
I Peter 1:16; 2:21, 24a; 4:12
II John 10-11
Jude 4
Revelation 21:4-5

DAY 20
II Timothy 1:6

DAY 21
Genesis 1:11-12

DAY 22
Philippians 3:17-18
Hebrews 12:13

DAY 23
Colossians 2:8
II John 10-11

DAY 24
Hebrews 6:4a, 6a; 10:24-25

DAY 25
Matthew 7:15-16a
Jude 4

DAY 26
Ruth 2:17
I Corinthians 15:58

DAY 27
Psalms 61:2
I Peter 4:12

DAY 28
Ephesians 6:1-3
I Peter 1:16

DAY 29
Matthew 10:34-36
II Timothy 4:9-10a, 11a

DAY 30
Philippians 1:21, 23
Revelation 21:4-5